How to value stock – a guide to industry practices

# How to value stock – a guide to industry practices

Editor

J. H. F. Gemmell, CA

The Institute of Chartered Accountants
in England and Wales
Chartered Accountants' Hall, Moorgate Place
London EC2P 2BJ
1983

In publishing this book, the Accounting Principles and Auditing Panel of The Institute of Chartered Accountants in England and Wales considers that it is a worthwhile contribution to discussion, without necessarily sharing the views expressed, which are those of the authors.



ISBN 0 85291 347 8



Typeset in 10/12 Photon Times
Printed in England by Staples St Albans Limited
at the Priory Press, Hertfordshire

# CONTENTS

# AUTHORS

The authors of the chapters are as set out below:

Editor:

| | |
|---|---|
| J. H. F. Gemmell, CA | Partner, Clark Whitehill |

Authors:

| | |
|---|---|
| J. C. Bell, FCA | Partner, Spicer & Pegler |
| G. C. C. Capon, FCA | Partner, Touche Ross & Co |
| M. S. Carnwath, FCA | Senior Manager, Peat, Marwick Mitchell & Co |
| D. W. Davis, FCA | Partner, Clark Whitehill |
| M. K. Down, FCA | Partner, Edward Moore & Sons |
| R. J. Fox, BSc (Econ), FCA | Technical and Training Director, Neville Russell |
| R. V. Gorlin, MA, FCA | Partner, Arthur Andersen & Co |
| S. Ingram, BA (Econ), FCA | Partner, Thornton Baker |
| D. R. Philip, FCA | Partner, Robson Rhodes |
| C. R. Plummer, CA | Partner, Deloitte Haskins & Sells |
| E. M. W. Robson, MA, FCA | Partner, Robson Rhodes |
| D. I. Stewart, BSc (Econ), ACA | Audit Manager, Thornton Baker |
| P. M. M. Taylor, FCA | Partner, Ernst & Whinney |

# PREFACE

This book emerged from a suggestion that accountants and businessmen should have a source from which they might familiarise themselves with a range of industries.

The suggestion developed into a proposal – this book – that a record of experiences in different industries, trades and professions should be prepared so that a reader could glean a brief background to specific industries; their accounting and auditing problems and any tax peculiarities.

Assembling a team of expert authors and co-operative technical monitors for a work such as this requires greater time than this editor anticipated. The authors displayed enormous patience with an editor who took nearly three years to execute his task. I can only express my admiration for the determination, perseverance and technical competence of the dozen who survived the course. The merits of this book are entirely theirs – the weaknesses must be the editor's who determined the framework within which the authors were constrained.

It is normal for editors to note that the views expressed in this work are not those of his firm. It is less usual, but nevertheless necessary, to state that the individual chapters do not represent the views of the individual authors' firms. I deemed it inappropriate to call a committee meeting of the authors and accordingly each author can only blame me and the other 11 for the balance of the book!

I should like to acknowledge the unfailing help and good humour which Donald A. R. Broad, BA (Econ), FCA, Technical Manager of Clark Whitehill and Deputy Technical Director of Clark Whitehill Associates Limited, has contributed to this work. Donald undertook much of the basic organisation and editing of this book. To him my grateful thanks.

25 New Street Square
London EC4A 3LN
September 1983

James Gemmell

# INTRODUCTION

The publication of SSAP 9 in May 1975 caused significant protests among those for whom the standard's inclusion of production and other attributable overheads (on manufactured stock) and attributable profit (on long-term contracts) represented a distinctly less prudent view than they had hitherto taken. Now, eight years on, the protests have to a certain degree abated, although there are still a number of voluble exceptions.

This book seeks to examine in relation to a dozen different industries:

(a) how SSAP 9 has been applied in the past eight years;
(b) what accounting and auditing problems have been encountered; and
(c) how these problems have been resolved.

As will be seen in the ensuing chapters, stocks comprise a wide variety of categories including not only manufactured goods but also, for example, holes in ground, cattle, wheat and time.

SSAP 9 was written at a time when 'no area of accounting has produced wider differences in practice than . . . the amount at which stocks and work-in-progress are stated in financial accounts' (SSAP 9). Stock valuation has always been a difficult and sometimes a contentious area. Its importance is not so much the balance-sheet aspect of valuation but its impact on the measurement of profit.

Nowadays the principles of SSAP 9 are enshrined in law. The Companies Act 1981 set out a number of detailed rules for valuing assets including stock. There is one area, however, where the law and the standard diverge – long-term contracts. The standard provides for attributable profit to be included; the Act provides for such profit to be excluded. The difficulties caused by this divergence of view are considered elsewhere in this book (see Chapter 4).

It seems at present that SSAP 9 is not to be subject to review for some time. Its application in the reality of commercial life is subject to the constraints of the various practices and backgrounds of different industries. Thus, for some years to come, accountants and others interested in the valuation of stocks will encounter problems in industries unfamiliar to them. It is hoped that the chapters of this book will provide a background and basis on which that unfamiliarity can be reduced; once that has happened part of the problems encountered will have diminished.

# ADVERTISING AGENCIES

R. V. Gorlin

**1.01** For many accountants the words 'stock' or 'work-in-progress' are not immediately associated with the advertising industry. However, a review of the balance sheet of a typical agency will reveal a caption described as work in progress or unbilled client costs. The purpose of this chapter is briefly to discuss the accounting for the costs incurred during the preparation of an advertisement by an agency and the associated audit problems. To appreciate the nature of this 'work-in-progress' a knowledge of the operations of an advertising agency is required and hence the first section of this chapter is given to providing such background information.

## Background to the business

**1.02** Advertising agencies are service organisations which develop, prepare and place advertising in advertising media such as newspapers, magazines, radio and television. These functions are carried out for specific clients who entrust the agency with the preparation and implementation of their advertising plans and thus a key function within an agency is that of account handling. Personnel involved in this area have responsibility for all phases of client contact including presenting agency recommendations, ensuring that all work for the client is carried out when required and that the account is operating within the approved budget. In essence, this function is one of liaison with the client and in-house departments with the objective of ensuring that the client's account is fully serviced.

**1.03** The organisational structure of agencies is variable but three departments which exist in most medium to large-sized agencies are described below.

### *Creative department*

**1.04** This department is involved with the actual preparation of advertising material and encompasses such activities as:

(a) the initiation of basic advertising themes, and the writing of all advertising material;

(b) the preparation and creation of layouts for advertisements. The finished artwork which goes into making a plate or mat is often handled by outside contractors;

(c) responsibility for controlling the mechanical production of advertisements.

*Media department*

**1.05** It is the responsibility of the media department to determine in which media the client can most advantageously spend his advertising budget. Once this has been decided, the question of selection of individual newspapers, magazines, radio stations, television contractors etc. is considered.

**1.06** The results of the above decisions are then forwarded to buyers who are generally identified by the media in which they specialise, e.g. television and press. Media plans will be drawn up and the appropriate bookings made after client approval has been obtained.

*Research department*

**1.07** This department is primarily engaged in the determination of the effectiveness of advertising. The department will have a number of outside research organisations to which it may turn for data to measure the effectiveness of advertising campaigns, or it may perform its own tests.

**1.08** A further function of the department will be to gather and analyse published statistics as they relate to agency clients and competitors. This information can be used as the basis for agency recommendations in media or advertising strategy.

*Remuneration basis*

**1.09** Traditionally, advertising agencies have been remunerated on a commission basis whereby a commission percentage is applied to all costs incurred by an agency on a client's behalf. The commission percentage and details of costs to be recharged with commission will be subject to the agreement reached with each individual client.

**1.10** As an alternative to the commission system, an agency may negotiate a set fee for servicing a client's account. Under this system, costs recharged to a client bear no mark-up.

**Production costs**

**1.11** Typical costs to be incurred include artist fees, block-making costs, artwork, photographic costs, studio fees and certain incidental costs, e.g. transportation. A major factor, besides the type of advertising involved, which determines the level of production costs recorded in any agency's books is the billing arrangements adopted with its clients. The two most common billing methods are:

(a) *Completed job basis.* The client is billed actual accumulated costs when the job is completed.

(b) *Progress billing.* Under this method a flat amount or a fixed percentage of estimated spend is billed at various stages during the preparation of the advertisement. Frequently costs for the production of a television advertisement will be paid in two phases (50 per cent before 'shooting' begins and 50 per cent on completion) and thus the agency may bill the client in a similar manner.

Consequently the level of 'work-in-progress' at any one time will depend on the billing arrangement agreed.

**Accounting for production costs**

**1.12** The accounting for production costs is relatively straightforward. The basic purpose of any production system is to accumulate billable client costs in connection with the production of advertisements. These costs are normally accumulated by job and hence the cost-accumulation process is similar to a job-costing system in a manufacturing company with each advertisement made by an agency given a separate job number.

**1.13** In small agencies the physical accumulation of costs is often achieved using a job-bag system whereby copies of suppliers' invoices and other support for expenditure incurred, relating to a given advertisement, are filed in one folder. The outside of the folder may be used to provide space for keeping a running total of costs incurred to date. Prior to processing any expenditure relating to production work the allocation to a job number would be approved by the account executive, the agency person who is responsible for the particular advertising account. For accounting purposes a subsidiary ledger should be set up with a ledger account for each job number. Monthly analysis of the purchase-day book and the main and petty cash books of the charges relating to each job are entered into the subsidiary ledger. The subsidiary ledger should then be reconciled to a control account in the general ledger.

**1.14** In larger agencies the above system would be mechanised and the subsidiary ledger replaced by a printout of unbilled costs by job number. Most computer printouts give some indication of the ageing of the accumulated costs. Some of the larger agencies have in-house computer facilities but the majority of medium to smaller size agencies employ one of several computer bureaux which specialise in accounting packages for advertising agencies; one such package will relate to the accumulation of production costs and the related billing function.

**Valuation of unbilled client costs**

**1.15** In most agencies unbilled client costs are stated at cost and no recognition is taken of the profit factor attributable to the work which will be realised when a billing is made. A few agencies, however, value work in progress at actual cost plus attributable profit. In these cases the attributable profit would reflect a percentage of the normal commission the agency expects to make on its production work. No profit should be taken on progress billings where the amount of the billing does not reflect the work actually done.

*Audit problems*

**1.16** Unbilled production costs reflect future debtors of the agency and hence the auditor's main concern is that these costs are billable and will be collected. In essence the auditor must establish that:

(a) The accumulated costs are *prima facie* rechargeable costs, and are allocated to the correct job number.

(b) The costs are being recharged on a timely basis and appropriate provisions are being provided against balances which are not able to be billed.

The first point requires little expansion as a review of underlying documentation and a knowledge of the agreement with the client should be sufficient to cover this area. The audit work required in connection with the second point is more complex and does require some form of analysis of unbilled production costs, preferably with a indication of the ageing. While reviewing such analyses, consideration should be given the factors set out below.

**1.17** If any agency renders progress billings to clients, the resulting credit entry will normally appear on the unbilled production ledger and hence reduce actual accumulated costs. This should be borne in mind especially when the agency is being held to a tight budget by the client and the auditor is attempting to estimate whether costs to date are in line with budget or whether there is a possibility of costs exceeding budget.

**1.18** The auditor is also interested in ensuring that where advance billings or *pro-forma* billings are made at the client's request, they have been correctly treated from an accounting standpoint. These should not be taken to gross billings and where little or no work has been done, it may be appropriate to reclassify such items out of 'work-in-progress' into 'creditors'.

**1.19** If a manual ageing only is available there may often be 'contra' debit and credit balances on a given job number where costs are accumulated in one month and billed in a different period, the client failing to match the two transactions correctly. A similar situation may arise where agencies have more than one job number for a given advertisement. It is possible for the majority of costs to be accumulated in one job number and all credits (arising from billings) in a second job number. Obviously such contra debits and credits should be identified and matched before the aged analysis can be reviewed meaningfully.

**1.20** Where agencies adopt a billing procedure not based on actual costs incurred and fail to make the correct adjustment on the final billing, it is possible for credit or debit balances to arise which represent the excess of billings made over actual charges incurred or vice versa. This situation may arise where clients set up provisions for costs to come, in order to bill clients on a prompt and regular basis. A consistent policy should be adopted for taking these debit and credit balances to the profit and loss account.

**1.21** While reviewing the analysis of unbilled costs, the auditor should ask whether any of the job numbers relate to the accumulation of costs of new client presentations. It is normal practice for these costs to be borne by the agency and hence they should be written off.

**1.22** Attention should be given to all job numbers acting as suspense accounts, i.e. costs awaiting job numbers, costs awaiting decisions from executives as to whether they are to be charged to clients or not. These items should be discussed with appropriate management to ensure that they will be eventually billed.

**1.23** Due to the delay in processing invoices which is inherent in most agencies, the true value of the unbilled costs will normally be understated. Again this should be borne in mind where agency expenditure is subject to a client budget. Thus while accumulated costs appear to be under budget, when the appropriate portion of the unprocessed invoices is added to the job number, the budget may be exceeded and a write-off may need to be reflected in the financial statements of the current year.

**1.24** Three further points should be considered when auditing unbilled production costs:

(a) *Determination of a correct sales cut-off.* Have costs been correctly relieved from work-in-progress for each billing made? This problem is usually more common in smaller agencies operating manual systems. If this has been identified as an audit problem, then specific audit tests will have to be designed.

(b) *Timing of production billings.* By delaying or bringing forward production billings at the financial year-end an agency can switch commission income between accounting periods. Obviously it is desirable that an agency adopts a uniform billing policy through the year. A review of the level of work-in-progress and production billing either side of the year-end and a knowledge of the agency's clients and their peak advertising periods may indicate whether the above problem exists.

(c) *Review of debit balances in creditors' ledger.* These sometimes arise because of poor accounting systems when the purchase is paid but the invoice is not processed and the corresponding charging of the cost to the production ledger is not processed either. In these situations it may often be too late, when the matter is discovered, to bill these items to the client with the result that they have to be written off.

# BREWERIES
## P. M. M. Taylor

---

**Background to the business**

**2.01** The brewing industry is an industry steeped in tradition. Many of the well-known brewing names trace their origins back to the sixteenth century. At the turn of the present century, the structure of the industry was highly fragmented and localised. Large numbers of brewers supplying a small market area were scattered throughout the country. This was largely due to the perishable nature of the product and the difficulty of transport. Technological changes in methods of brewing and preserving beer, increase in the capacity of plant and improved transport have encouraged the merger and rationalisation of many of the old companies so that the number of companies actively brewing has diminished from some four thousand in 1914 to eight at the present day.

**2.02** These remaining companies now fall broadly into two categories:

(a) *Brewers with tied estates.* These are brewers who, in addition to brewing, both wholesale their beer and also own a substantial proportion of the retail outlets they supply.

(b) *Brewers without tied estates.* These are the companies which are solely brewers. They normally sell in bulk to other brewers who in turn retail it through their own tied outlets or through independent retailers, known as the free trade. The companies in this category account for approximately 13 per cent of the beer market in this country and the best-known example is Guinness.

**2.03** The brewers with tied estates can be further categorised among national companies, regional companies and small brewers. The national companies comprise groups such as Allied Breweries, Bass, Whitbread, Scottish and Newcastle, Watney Truman and Courage. The last two are now part of major groups outside the brewing industry. These national groups brew beer, distribute it and sell it in their own public houses and off-licences and also act as wholesalers selling to independent retailers. They operate, as the name implies, throughout the UK and account between them for some 70 per cent of the beer market in this country.

**2.04** Regional brewers comprise companies such as Boddingtons, Matthew Brown, Greenall Whitley, Greene King, Vaux Brewers and Wolver hampton and Dudley. They operate in much the same way but on a regional scale, and account for approximately seven per cent of the UK market.

**2.05** The above is a brief outline of the structure of the industry and indicates that, because the industry controls its retail outlets either by direct management or through the tied-house system whereby the brewers' tenants have to buy their liquor from the brewery, companies are not only involved in the manufacture and sale of beer but also in the provision of the other products sold in public houses. They are usually concerned therefore with the manufacture of soft drinks and minerals and the factoring of wines and spirits, cider and tobacco, and the supply of the necessary equipment needed in their outlets to bring the product to the point of sale. The main trading stocks are considered below.

**Beer stock**

**2.06** The manufacture of beer is essentially a simple process. The basic raw materials in all beers are hops, malt, sugar and water. The malt is ground to a fine flour called grist. This is then deposited into a mash tun, mixed with water (referred to in the trade as liquor) at a certain temperature and allowed to stand for a few hours. The mixture, known as wort, is then run off through perforations in the bottom of the mash tun into coppers, leaving the grains in the mash which are sold off as cattle food. Hops and sugar are then added to the wort in the coppers and the mixture is boiled for between one and three hours.

After boiling, the wort is passed into a hop back which acts as a strainer to separate the spent hops from the clean hopped wort. The wort is then cooled in a refrigeration plant prior to passing into the fermenting vessels. At this stage, the brew is declared and the liquor is gauged by the Customs and Excise officer to determine the specific gravity and volume of the beer on which duty is payable by the brewer.

Yeast is added in the fermenting vessels and the beer is left for four to five days for fermentation to occur. During the fermentation the yeast rises in a frothy mass to the top of the liquid and is skimmed off for use on future occasions. The remaining liquid – beer – is then ready for casking or passing into conditioning tanks prior to bottling, canning or kegging. Thus, at any cut-off date, stock to be evaluated falls into the following categories:

(a) raw materials;

(b) beer in process;

(c) finished beer in containers.

*Raw materials*

**2.07** *Malt.* In the past brewers often operated their own maltings. This is now uncommon and malt is usually bought in from specialist maltings. Each autumn, the brewer will negotiate contracts with the maltsters to supply his needs over the following year. The contracts are usually fixed price with escalation clauses. The brewery keeps detailed stock records of malt purchased by type and usage and these records are available for inspection by the Customs and Excise officer at any time.

**2.08** *Hops.* Most brewers buy hops from hop factors acting as agents for the growers. The price is fixed at the time of harvest and the brewer estimates his needs at least for the following year. The hops are usually kept in cold storage by the merchant and drawn by the brewer as and when required. The brewer's quantity records are again kept meticulously to record hops purchased and usage in each brew. Periodic physical counts of hops on the premises and those held by third parties should reconcile with the book records maintained. Small variances can be expected due to the moisture content in the hops.

These variances, however, have been largely eradicated by the use of hop extracts and the pelletisation of hops whereby the brewer nominates the hops he requires which are then sent to merchants for crushing and converting to hop pellets. This allows the brewer greater storage capacity and easier physical count as the pellets are packed in neat boxes or plastic bags. It also allows for easier reconciliation between book and physical stock.

Hops are valued by type at the prices agreed in the contract and audit of the evaluation again poses few problems. However, hops are usually paid for by instalments, a deposit at the time of order in October or November of each year and the balance plus storage charges when hops are delivered to the brewery. It is important to ensure that the full price, where not paid, is included as a creditor at the year-end date as well as in stock.

**2.09** *Sugar.* This is used as an additive to the beer in greater or lesser quantities according to the type of beer. Detailed records are again kept by the brewer by type of sugar purchased and used in each brew and the records are controlled on a sample basis by the Customs and Excise. Deliveries of sugar to the brewery are accompanied by a formal weighbridge ticket identifying volume deliveries. This is a requirement of the Excise Acts since the strength of beer can be increased by the addition of priming sugars during the fermentation stage and after duty has been levied by the Excise office. Thus, this is an added control on the quantity movements and the stock records maintained by the brewery. As with the other raw materials, sugar will be valued by type at invoice price.

*Beer in process*

**2.10** Most brewers have fairly sophisticated stock-control systems in which they record the movements of each brew during the brewing process. Records are maintained by the brewer showing, for each brew, the quantity of materials used, the liquor added and the resulting volume of beer as gauged by the Customs and Excise which starts in the fermenting vessels and flows through to the finished product in casks, bottles or other containers. In the measurement and auditing of quantities of beer in process in fermenting vessels and tanks at the stocktake date, it is important that these records are used to follow up the test counts, particularly where the exact quantity cannot be ascertained because gauges may not be working properly and it is not easy for the untutored eye to ascertain the quantity being dealt with.

**2.11** Evaluation of the material and duty cost of beer in process is also carried out by the brewer for each brew. Excise duty is levied at the stage where the beer goes into the fermenting vessel. The Excise officer dips the beer in the fermenting vessel and gauges the volume by barrel and specific gravity. The volume is agreed to the brewer's records and duty is levied accordingly. Because the duty is levied at this early stage of production, an allowance of six per cent of the duty payable is made to take account of losses of beer through fermentation and packaging.

**2.12** Thus, the material and duty cost of beer in process at the cut-off date is available in the brewer's records for each brew and can be tested by reference to invoice price in respect of materials used and by reference to official duty tables published by Customs and Excise for duty.

**2.13** In an average barrel of bitter, raw materials would account for approximately 10 per cent of total cost and duty approximately 60 per cent. The remaining 30 per cent would be the addition of production and handling costs. Materials and duty are therefore more important areas to consider when evaluating beer in process. The methods of allocating production costs, as with other industries, vary from brewer to brewer. Beer in process is usually valued at material and duty cost together with brewing production costs, labour, power, plant repairs, depreciation, etc, and examination of management accounts will show whether the overhead costs are reasonably allocated.

*Finished beer*

**2.14** As mentioned above, brewers keep records of each brew through the brewing process to the finished product in casks or other containers. They also keep records of beer by type showing what has been produced, what sold and the stock still on the premises awaiting sale. In counting stock at the cut-off date, it is important to ensure that stock held at all locations is covered so that agreement with these records can be made. Many brewers have production centres from where the finished product is transported either in containers or in bulk to distribution depots to be stored prior to sale. Because of the size of the containers, counting stock poses few problems. However, the normal procedures for segregating stocks which are awaiting delivery must be observed and because bottled beer in cases is usually stored in pallet loads of a standard number on each pallet, it is important to ensure by test that pallet loads are not in fact 'hollow squares'.

The basic evaluation of beer is by reference to material, duty and overhead cost already considered under 'Beer in process'. There will be other costs to add depending on the type of container the finished product is in, i.e., bottles, cans or kegs. The cost of non-returnable containers is taken in the evaluation at this stage but beer in returnable containers is evaluated at material, duty and process cost in putting the beer into the container, returnable containers being accounted for separately. Most brewers also hold stocks of beer bought from other brewers for distribution through their own outlets. This 'foreign' beer would normally be evaluated at invoice price.

**Wines and spirits in stocks**

**2.15** An integral part of the brewery industry is the wines and spirits trade. All breweries are involved in this trade to a greater or lesser extent. It is mainly a factoring operation, although many breweries now operate as producers and blenders of spirits either individually or through associated companies owned jointly with other brewers. Some have extensive wine-importing interests and ship wines in bulk, bottling (particularly in the low to medium-price range) under their own lables. One of the advantages to the industry from their participation in the wine and spirit market is that they can buy in bulk in the necessary quantities to meet the demands of their own outlets which enables them to obtain good discounts. There is also the advantage of the economy that can be made by the use of a common distribution system for beers, wines and spirits.

**2.16** Wines and spirits stock holdings fall into two categories. They are either in bond or duty paid. Imported wines and spirits and spirits produced in this country are initially held in bonded warehouses until the appropriate excise duty has been paid. The bonds are controlled by Customs and Excise and careful records are kept of stocks in bond which are checked by the Customs and Excise. Breweries frequently have their own bonded warehouses and store duty-free stocks in them until required for sale. They will then pay the necessary duty to release those stocks from bond.

From the audit point of view, it is important to ensure that stocks held in bond are accounted for whether they are brewery owned or third party owned. Certificates of such stocks held by third parties should be obtained and compared with stock records at the brewery. It is also important that these stocks are separately identified for evaluation purposes so that the correct price is used. Duty-paid price applied to stocks held in bond will result in a gross over-valuation of stock because, as with beers, excise duty on wines and spirits is the greatest element of cost. Stocks held in bond are usually evaluated at invoice price on a FIFO basis.

**2.17** Because wines and spirits are high-value products and often require time to mature, the investment tied up in stock is relatively high. Many brewers have held large quantities of fine wines but in the last few years, in order to cut this investment in stocks and to meet consumer demand, the larger companies particularly have reduced the number of lines maintained in stock to the cheaper and fast-moving brands. One such company carried out this reduction in fairly drastic terms by holding a wine sale. The effect of this was to depress the value of many fine wines to the extent that some other companies holding high stocks of these wines which had been purchased on a rising market found that the realisable value of some of the stocks was less than cost and were forced to make the necessary provision on their stock evaluations. Although prices of fine wines have strengthened considerably, the auditor, in assessing the valuation of maturing wines must always have regard to their realisable value.

### Stocks in retail outlets

**2.18** The largest market for brewers' products is through the tied trade where the brewery owns the freehold of the public house or off-licence and lets the premises to a licensee who is 'tied' to the brewery for the purchase of beers, wines, spirits, etc. on sale in the house. In these circumstances, the brewer acts only as a wholesaler, the tenant or licensee taking the retail margin. However, brewery companies increasingly now also manage many of their retail outlets. They then take not only the wholesale profit but the retail profit as well. Stock at managed houses can therefore form a significant part of the brewing company's stocks.

Stocks are counted at managed houses, usually on a monthly cycle, by stocktakers employed by the brewery. By recording purchases by house and evaluating sales by product, a comparison is made between the cash actually taken by house during the period and the amount which should have been taken. Allowances are made for differing pricing structures in various areas of the house and, after these allowances, the two figures should be similar.

The results of these stocktakes by house are carefully monitored because they are used in cases of consistently bad results to dismiss the manager who bears a responsibility for the stock movements in his house. The auditor, by a scrutiny of the monthly and cumulative stock results can quickly see the efficiency or otherwise of the stock-control system in force in relation to retail outlets, where the problem areas are, and how they are dealt with. It is also necessary to ensure that the stocktakers employed by the brewer do not always attend the same houses as a prevention of collusion between stocktaker and manager.

**2.19** At the year-end, the auditor will probably attend a selection of the managed houses with the stocktaker to observe the count. Because of the number of outlets involved, stocks cannot be counted at all managed houses on the cut-off date. The stock is therefore usually taken as near the period end as possible and updated by an adjustment for goods delivered to the house and sales by the house between the stocktake and cut-off date. This adjustment can be tested for accuracy by reference to delivery notes and cash returns from the house between the two dates in question. Goods sold to the managed houses by the brewery are normally at brewery wholesale price and evaluated at that price in arriving at the managed house stock and profits. When consolidating this stock into the brewery company accounts, there is therefore an element of unrealised profit to be eliminated from the stock evaluation in respect of stocks on hand purchased from the brewery to reduce these stocks to cost. This adjustment is usually made by deducting the wholesale profit margin from the overall analysis by category of managed house stocks.

## Returnable containers

**2.20** A significant proportion of a brewer's investment in stock is tied up in containers. The brewer's products are packaged either in casks, kegs, bottles or cases. Cases and kegs are generally regarded as fixed assets and accounted for as such. This is traditional because a certain amount of conditioning occurs in the cask. Some bottles and cases are disposable and expensed as part of the cost of production and do not therefore concern us here. However, the majority of bottles and cases are charged out to customers at deposit rate and credited on return at the same rate, the movements of these containers both full and empty between suppliers and customers being accounted for separately from the products they contain.

There are several methods of accounting for containers and problems arise because of the volume of transactions involved and because many cases and bottles are of standard size and can be interchanged between different breweries. The method for accounting for containers and controls over issues and returns should therefore be given careful consideration. All methods of accounting for returnable containers, however, involve the assessment of stocks both full and empty at the balance sheet date at the brewery premises and in customer's hands.

When testing the count at brewery premises the auditor should watch for the 'hollow squares' mentioned above. Stocks in customers' hands are usually assessed by examining the returns for a certain number of days after the year-end and including these in the valuation matched by a liability to repurchase containers of the same amount. The number of days selected will vary between breweries and depends upon the delivery pattern but will usually be in the region of 14 days. The auditor should examine the basis used to ensure that the assessment fits the normal delivery pattern of the brewery and is consistent with previous years. Stocks of returnable containers are usually included in the balance sheet at deposit rate and the values will be verified by normal audit procedures.

# CHEMICALS

M. S. Carnwath

## Background to the business

**3.01** The size and scope of the chemicals industry needs little explanation for there are few aspects of our daily lives on which the use of chemicals does not impinge. A glance at the categories into which official government statistics relating to the chemicals industry are broken (e.g. pharmaceuticals, toilet preparations, paint, soap) indicates the effect that the industry has on our lives.

**3.02** The chemicals industry is often taken by analysts as a good indicator of the health of the economy since its products form the base for so many processes. It is particularly affected by energy costs and, during 1979, the cost of materials and fuel purchased by the industry rose sharply to a level some 22 per cent higher than the previous year. Import costs rose faster than those for manufacturing industry as a whole, reflecting the large increase in the price of oil and oil-related products on which the industry is so dependant.

**3.03** The chemical industry is in the main heavily capital intensive, with gross capital stock representing some 25 per cent of the total UK manufacturing industry. Stocks and work in progress amount to some 13 per cent of the total.

**3.04** Because of the wide variety of processes and types of stock holdings, it is not possible to write a comprehensive guide to the problems of valuing stock. It is true that normal accounting rules can be applied but it should be pointed out that a great degree of reliance necessarily has to be placed on the clients' staff particularly during the identification and physical counting of stock and on the commercial directors in the estimation of realisable value. The following sets out, on an exceptional basis, the areas the auditor should pay particular attention to in his audit of chemical company stocks.

## Stock quantities

**3.05** As with all companies, the auditor will need to satisfy himself that proper procedures and controls are in operation to ensure that there is no material over or understatement of stock quantities. In the normal course of events, this will comprise attendance at stocktaking, cut-off procedures and other routine audit checks. The chemical industry is no exception, but there are certain practical problems which, whilst not being unique to the chemical industry, do commonly arise.

*Identification*

**3.06** Under normal circumstances, it would be a reasonable assumption for the auditor to be able to identify physically materials produced by a given industry. However, in some cases, a chemical product can be made to an acceptable specification by substituting raw materials of a different description from those in the standard recipe. This situation may occur for instance where there is a temporary shortage of a particular raw material in the standard recipe and loss of production is avoided by using a substitute. Since it is not uncommon to book out of stock by reference to the standard constituents of the finished products produced, this can lead to substantial stock differences in raw materials. Thus if the physical stocktake is some way before the year-end with adjustment to year-end figures by reference to book movements, enquiries should be made whether any large degree of substitution of raw materials has taken place.

**3.07** There may also be instances where independent analysis may be required, since, in the case of the chemical industry, a large proportion of stocks held will not be readily identifiable to the layman. As a consequence, thorough investigation will be required of the clients' systems for controlling the storage and segregation of stock, backed up by independent analyses of selected items. In this regard, it should be noted that in, for example, the fine chemicals sector where newly-researched chemicals are being produced to specific order, an independent analysis may prove unduly expensive, if not impossible. In these circumstances, the auditor may wish to consider the possibility of selecting items at random, and in secret, for analysis by the company's own chemists.

*Physical quantities*

**3.08** Whilst much of the stock may be conveniently stored in bags, clearly marked as to identity and weight, it will not be unusual for chemicals to be stockpiled or in tanks. In addition, large quantities of stock will be in work-in-progress.

**3.09** Stockpiles present particular problems. There is no doubt that, if large quantities held in stockpiles have to be measured, there is no substitute for keeping book records of the quantity put in a particular pile and the quantity removed from that pile and then proceeding on the basis of exhausting specific piles and writing off any resultant book difference in respect of that pile.

**3.10** In practice, most chemical companies will have difficulty in maintaining a regular and accurate quantity record of such stock as issues into production are seldom measured. Only theoretical issues are normally available, which are derived by applying a usage factor to the quantity of finished product. The actual usage is only known to the company when a physical inspection of the raw material is made by surveyors. The auditor therefore has to ensure that such stocks are surveyed at regular intervals and can place little reliance on the book quantities.

**3.11** The following two paragraphs detail the facts of an actual occurrence and the steps that were taken to avoid any repetition. It will be seen that, in certain circumstances, independent verification procedures are no substitute for detailed knowledge of the product which will be found amongst the client's staff.

**3.12** This particular case involved a stock write-down of some 3,000 tonnes of a product which represented three per cent of total annual production. The penultimate stage in the manufacturing process involved the filtration of a thick slurry to produce a product which contains around 10 per cent moisture. This product was then either sold as such or dried and then despatched to customers. The product was generally stored in a warehouse but at times of high stock levels, quantities were stored outside in discrete stockpiles, sheeted to prevent losses and moisture. One of the problems associated with this particular product was that whilst the volume of stock could be assessed accurately, the density and the moisture content could vary and, consequently, the total weight of stock, despite accurate volume measurements, also varied.

Considerable care had been taken by the company to ensure accurate measurements. All production passed over a continuous weigh-belt which provided a reasonable assessment of daily output. This production value was compared, on a daily basis, with measurements of despatches and assessments of both moist and dry product stock. Once a month, the stock quantities were checked against an accurate volume measurement taken by the company's surveying department. Despite the above procedures, it was discovered, during a run-down of stock levels, that quantity was overstated by some 3,000 tonnes. This arose principally because, in order to obtain the actual weight of stock, the already accurate volume measurements achieved above had to be associated with precise measurement of bulk density and moisture content.

**3.13** After considerable study, the company concluded that the only way of avoiding a repeat of the overstatement was periodically to move the stockpiles, load quantities onto vehicles and physically weigh the product. This, coupled with tube sampling over the stock to obtain samples in depth for moisture content measurement, provided accurate assessments but clearly resulted in substantial additional handling costs.

**3.14** In the case of materials stored in tanks there is a practical problem in that in many chemical processes the rate of usage is so high that the auditor should ensure that he is present when stocks are measured in order to avoid lengthy reconciliations to prove physical quantities. Close liaison is therefore required with the client's staff during the planning of the stocktake.

**3.15** There is a further problem where stock is liquid and held in substantial storage tanks. Some bulk-produced chemicals contain an impurity element which either floats up to the top of the tank or sinks to the bottom. A gauge reading from the particular tank concerned does not therefore identify the quantum of stock which may be unusable. The only remedy is to exhaust particular tanks periodically of usable product and thus identify the unusable product still contained in the tank.

**3.16** Difficulties may be experienced because of the nature of the chemical stored in tanks. For example, phosphorous ignites on contact with air so that it has to be stored under water. It has been the author's experience that, in these circumstances, stock quantities can only be identified accurately by arranging a run-out of all tanks prior to the year-end.

**3.17** It is seldom possible for an auditor to inspect physically the quantities of material in work-in-progress, in contrast to the ease with which this work can be done in the engineering industry. This is because the auditor is often dealing with a continuous chemical process which is uneconomic or impossible to close down for stocktaking purposes. There may be a large number of stages to the process and the weight of the end product may differ from the weight of the raw material input. The chemicals in process are, of course, largely invisible to the stocktaker and he may therefore have to rely either on a technical assessment of the quantity in process or on records giving quantity in process by deducting output from input or by gauge readings where the product is held in tanks at intermediate stages.

**3.18** In addition to the above, two further points should be borne in mind. Significant quantities of both raw materials and finished goods may be held off site, and frequently may be held abroad. In the case of finished goods these are often held by agents. The auditor needs to take steps to obtain certificates as to the physical existence of such stocks.

**3.19** The specification of chemical stocks must be to a very narrow tolerance. Analysis of sample materials is therefore an important part of the stock check. Also, it is quite common for materials to go off-specification quickly if proper storage is not given to them. This obviously is a matter which must be considered during the audit.

**Valuation and statement of standard accounting practice No. 9 (SSAP 9)**

**3.20** SSAP 9 requires that the amount at which stocks and work-in-progress, other than long-term contract work-in-progress, as stated in the periodic financial statements, should be the total of the lower of cost and net-realisable value of the separate items of stock and work-in-progress, or of groups of similar items.

**3.21** The internal costing methods are most important in establishing the cost of finished goods. The auditor needs to have confidence that the company's methods are reasonable and are consistently applied from year to year. There are no set methods for costing, and therefore each company will cost in a different manner. The auditor therefore needs to follow through in detail the cost of a product, starting with the prime production plant, through the various manufacturing stages, to the ultimate finished product. The auditor should pay close attention to the methods of accounting for inter/intra plant transfers and to the accounting treatment of by-products.

As an example of this latter point, some chemical processes such as the manufacturing of sulphuric acid, produce steam which is used for the generation of power and for high and low-pressure steam for other plants. In some costing methods steam may be transferred free from the sulphuric acid plant which makes the acid expensive, whilst in others the sulphuric acid may be credited with the calorific value of the steam which will reduce the cost of that acid. Consistency of approach in such cases, both between different sites in a company and from year to year, is material in the valuations adopted for stock.

**3.22** A high proportion of the final stock valuation is the fixed production cost element covering generally all process labour, supervision, management, quality control, insurance, rates and depreciation. The amount of the fixed costs included in the valuation will vary greatly with the volumes over which the fixed costs are absorbed into inventory. The Accounting Standard calls for such costs to be absorbed into inventory on the basis of normal capacity.

**3.23** The maintainable operating capacity of a chemical plant is a specialised subject and the auditor will have to satisfy himself by discussions with production and marketing directors that appropriate levels have been adopted for the computation of overhead recovery. In many chemical processes the essential design of plant may not change much, but small innovations (removing bottle necks in the plant, change of raw material mix) can materially alter the economic operating capacity of the plant.

**3.24** Problems of stock valuation arise where individual chemical plants are working at less than normal capacity owing either to a lack of demand for the product or else through a design fault leading to plant malfunction. In such cases difficult judgement decisions are necessary so as to ensure that cost of inefficiencies are not included in the stock valuation.

**3.25** Linked with the problem of assessing normal capacity is the high amount of maintenance cost associated with the corrosive atmosphere surrounding chemical plants and the fact that maintenance is seldom carried out on an even pattern throughout the year. The accounting methods adopted for maintenance should be fully understood and examined by the auditor.

**3.26** It needs to be emphasised that capacity is a critical area in the measurement of profit and that care should be taken to ensure that a realistic operating level is assumed so as to avoid distortion of results on a year-to-year basis.

**3.27** SSAP 9 defines net-realisable value as the amount which it is estimated will be realised from the disposal of stocks in the normal course of business, either in their existing condition or as incorporated in the products normally sold, after deducting all costs of completion and disposal. The general principle is that where there is evidence that realisable value is less than cost, the loss should be recognised in the period in which it becomes apparent. No additional provision should be made where replacement cost is less than realisable value so as to provide a margin on the disposal of stock in future periods.

**3.28** Many chemical products are high volume, low mark-up and have many of the characteristics of commodities with the rapidly fluctuating sale price that this implies. Market pressures may lead to different home and export prices and, where the industry is suffering from severe import competition and weak prices, careful attention may need to be paid by the auditor to net-realisable value calculations based on planned selling prices.

**3.29** Difficult judgemental problems on net-realisable value also arise where the product in question has a cost of production which fluctuates significantly owing to price movements in commodity raw materials. The situation can arise, for example, where raw material prices have fallen sharply prior to the year-end and are continuing to fall after the year-end at the time of the audit. It is unusual in these circumstances for the price of the finished product to fluctuate as markedly and rapidly as the price of the underlying raw materials, and the extent to which it will fluctuate is a function of the competition in the market between manufacturers of the finished product concerned. Generally the more the competition the greater the price sensitivity. If there has been 'bad buying' of commodity raw materials then significant provisions may be necessary against raw-materials stocks bought at high prices because future selling prices of the finished product may weaken.

**3.30** SSAP 9 requires that provision be made on an item-by-item basis. In this regard, it should be emphasised that a particular finished product may be produced in a variety of ways. In particular it may be possible to use differing mixes of raw materials, different raw materials and different processes to produce the same product. This will require consideration when computing a provision.

**3.31** In many instances, procurement of raw material feedstock may present problems to a chemical company. This may result for a number of reasons, for example where the feedstock is mined. In such circumstances it would not be unusual for the company to build strategic stocks of the raw material, which may at the year-end be large. As mentioned previously, the end product of a chemical process frequently has, from a marketing point of view, similar characteristics to goods dealt with on the commodities markets. In times of softening prices, it will be difficult for the directors to forecast with any degree of certainty likely selling prices beyond, say, six months from the year-end. This will inevitably lead to difficulty in deciding the appropriate sale price to be used in computing realisable values.

**3.32** There are certain other sundry points which the auditor may need to consider.

**3.33** Where production is particularly capital intensive, it is common practice for large volumes of plant spares to be held. This is because if a particular part of a plant fails, there could be significant delay and loss arising from the inability to replace rapidly the part concerned. However, a particular spare part may not be needed for many years and the auditors may therefore be faced with old slow-moving stocks, which may in fact never be used since technological change may cause a particular plant to be scrapped before it becomes necessary to use the spares held for it. It is a common practice to write-down stocks of such spares according to their age, using a predetermined standard formula.

**3.34** Some chemical compounds are not stable and deteriorate either with time or if not properly stored. In such cases provision may need to be made against stocks which are nearing the end of their 'shelf life'.

**3.35** Certain chemicals may have only small inherent value; for example a bottle full of chemical may be only marginally more valuable than the bottle. The auditor needs to be aware of such items to avoid undue wastage of time.

**3.36** Care will need to be given to the treatment of catalysts. Certain processes require a catalyst which has a long life and is extremely expensive. It may be appropriate in certain circumstances to treat such catalysts as forming part of the plant and to disclose them as fixed assets rather than stock.

**3.37** In conclusion, consideration needs to be given to three factors which are largely outside the control of the company;

(a) Energy costs;

(b) Technological change;

(c) Government control.

**3.38** It was stated at the beginning that the chemical industry is heavily dependent on oil. In a climate of rapidly fluctuating prices of oil, both as a raw material and energy input, consideration will have to be given to its impact on the realisable value of stocks on hand. Since many products are high volume, low mark-up, the only tangible guide will be the company's and the industry's previous success in passing on any additional costs.

**3.39** Technology changes will have to be examined for their own merits and a common-sense approach taken. For example, European governments have been pressing the public to use washing powders that operate in cold water and thus save energy. Common sense indicates that housewives are unlikely to buy new washing machines simply to use cold water and thus processes directed to hot-water washing may reasonably be considered safe.

**3.40** Government controls may be much more immediate in their impact. For example, the United States has banned the use of fluorocarbons in sprays although Europe has not. It is therefore recommended that general discussions be held with the directors of the company on such matters. The Chemical Industries Association is a powerful lobbying body and the standard of the information given out by them is normally high. However, it is also important that audit staff understand the uses to which the client's products are put – the best source of this information will be the client himself.

# CONSTRUCTION

G. C. C. Capon

## Background to the business

**4.01** Construction is an important sector of the economy which accounts for over 10 per cent of the UK Gross Domestic Product. It includes a wide range of activities, from civil engineering projects, such as the building of roads and bridges and the laying down of infrastructure, sewerage systems or power grids, to the erection of office and factory buildings and of domestic housing units. Repair and maintenance activities account for about a third of the construction total. Participants in the industry vary between international public companies and sole traders; throughout the remainder of the chapter the word 'company' is used to denote all such concerns, unless otherwise stated. Because of the wide variety of skills needed to complete a project, it is common for the main contractor to assign parts of the work, such as electrical wiring, glazing, etc., to specialist subcontractors.

**4.02** Much of manufacturing industry is concerned with the output of a large number of relatively homogeneous items which are held in store until sold. Although output levels are determined in relation to quantities which can be sold, production is often not directed at a particular customer. In contrast, the construction industry is usually concerned with one-off projects for a particular customer. A further distinction is that a very detailed contract is generally drawn up and agreed prior to commencement of work, and this sets out the detailed specifications of the project and the terms of sale.

**4.03** The general term 'construction' covers two types of activity, namely contract work and speculative or development work. A company may undertake to build an office block for a client. The company is contractually bound to carry out the project in accordance with the terms of the contract, and, correspondingly, the client is obliged to pay the company on the specified terms. From the company's point of view, there is no uncertainty as to the finding of a buyer for its work. This situation may be contrasted with that of another company which undertakes a housing development project, hoping to sell the completed houses to private purchasers; that company does not enjoy any certainty as to the existence of potential buyers. Of course, some companies undertake both types of activity.

**4.04** Throughout this chapter, the term 'contracting' is used when there is a contract, and 'construction' when there is no contract. The distinction between the two types of activity is important because accounting conventions differentiate between the methods used for valuation of, and the recognition of profits on, short-term contracts, long-term contracts and work which is not the subject of a contract. All construction work should be valued at cost or net realisable value, if lower. The valuation of contracting work will depend on whether it is long term or short term.

**4.05** A distinction can be made between subcontractors and main contractors. Generally subcontractors work consists of short-term contracts, of a fairly standard and repetitive nature apart, perhaps, from civil engineering and major building contracts, which will probably be long term; whereas with main contractors, the work is more likely to be long term.

**4.06** One of the features of the industry's work is that it is mainly carried out on site (although modern pre-fabrication methods may reduce the extent of work performed on site in some cases). The figure stated in a contractor's balance sheet as work-in-progress represents a physical asset, but not one which he owns without restriction; it represents the value of work done for which in his opinion he has a right to be paid. Whereas a manufacturer owns his work-in-progress, the partly completed work of a contractor is often owned by the owner of the underlying land, although it will be reflected in the contractor's balance sheet. The nature of a contractor's work-in-progress therefore is basically that of an amount which he believes is due from his client.

**4.07** The involvement in distinct, material projects which are usually started and finished in different accounting periods, would probably result in considerable fluctuations of reported earnings if contracting companies were to apply the normal manufacturing industry practice of valuing inventory at cost. The latter, when applied in the industry, is commonly referred to as the 'completed contracts' method. Its main weakness in the context of reporting profits is that its application results in a year's profits reflecting the incidence of job completions, rather than the level of activity carried out during the year. On the other hand, it is certainly a prudent concept. The alternative basis known as 'the percentage of completion' method, involves the recognition of a proportion of estimated total profits in the valuation of work-in-progress, and results in a more regular and arithmetically based recognition of net income.

**4.08** It is important that the fundamental concept of prudence is not jeopardised when the percentage of completion method is used. Also the choice between the two methods must reflect actual circumstances. The claim of prudence to being the more important consideration is strengthened by the fact that the industry has traditionally been a high risk/low profit margin sector of the economy. In some cases, businesses are engaged in contracts, the outcome of which is subject to so many uncertainties, that the eventual result will not be determinable until after completion of the contract. In such cases it is clearly incorrect to take profits before completion.

**4.09** Official pronouncements of generally accepted accounting principles consist in the UK of SSAP 9 and internationally of IAS No. 11. The American Institute of Certified Public Accountants (AICPA) issued an Audit and Accounting Guide – *Construction Contractors* in July 1981 which superseded the 1955 *Accounting Research Bulletin No. 45*. Included in the guide was a proposal to the Financial Accounting Standards Board entitled *Statements of Position 81–1, Accounting for Performance of construction-type and certain production-type contracts*, which covers not only traditional construction-type activities, but also the newer activities in high technology fields. FASB 56, issued in February 1982, effectively endorsed these proposals.

**4.10** With the spread of activity, geographically and in increasingly more complex technology, it is becoming common for companies to join together as joint ventures, associated companies or partnerships, not only to spread the huge risks involved but also to pool specialised knowledge and thus to improve their competitive edge. Such joint ventures need special care in detail at all stages, particularly planning, staffing, consideration of tax aspects and accounting.

**Types of stocks held**

**4.11** The relative proportions of the three main elements of stocks (materials, work-in-progress, and finished goods) differ in the industry from those encountered in most other sectors of manufacturing. In the case of a constructor, the gross value of work-in-progress is nearly always a most significant balance. There will usually be no finished items awaiting sale except in the case of constructors.

**4.12** In the case of construction companies which engage in property development, including housing, there is another element, namely land. This will rarely have been purchased for a single job though, and accordingly will usually be treated as stock and valued at the lower of cost and net realisable value. The value of such land can be dependent on the progress of negotiations for planning permission from local authorities, as well as on a variety of other market conditions, including interest rates. The estimation of net realisable value therefore needs to be approached with care, and after taking into account all relevant circumstances. When development starts on a project transfers are made from the land account to work-in-progress.

**4.13** In some cases land may be purchased which does not have outline planning permission, on the basis of 'hope value' for future development and at a cost in excess of its alternative use value. The land should be written down to its market value if outline planning permission is not granted, but even when negotiations for outline (and thereafter detailed) planning permission are in progress, estimates of net realisable value should be revised in the light of anticipated delays in the eventual development. Such estimates should take account of actual interest costs of holding the land until development commences.

**4.14** Some development companies capitalise the cost of interest incurred on borrowings used to finance the purchase of land and its subsequent development. Interest should not be capitalised beyond the time at which development is complete, and care must be taken to ensure that interest capitalisation does not result in the carrying value of the land exceeding net realisable value. Completion may not be physical completion in this context but could be when the development reaches a certain (predetermined) letting point. Some accountants and developers believe that capitalisation of interest on land held specifically for sale is not justifiable, and only interest attributable to land not held for resale should be capitalised. There is a practical problem in applying such a rule in that a company may subsequently decide to sell land initially bought for development.

**4.15** A variety of different materials is used in construction projects. The physical and accounting control of such disparate materials as aggregates, steel girders, copper wire, and consumable items is a major problem. The problems of physical control are particularly acute because materials tend to be dispersed round the site.

**4.16** In principle, materials should be valued at the lower of cost and net realisable value; the latter being that which will be realised by incorporation into the relevant project, and not by resale. The terms of the contract require examination because they may provide that materials delivered to site constitute the client's property. In such cases there is no distinction between materials on site which have been used for work-in-progress, and those which have not.

**4.17** Some contractors adopt the same approach to materials in their own site records and charge the cost of all materials on site to a single work-in-progress account. This practice can result in profit being recognised too soon under the percentage of completion method, and is not recommended. If separate stock records are not maintained for unutilised materials on site, an estimate of their value should be made and transferred from the work-in-progress account to a materials stock account at the accounting date.

**Costs to be allocated to work-in-progress**

**4.18** The materiality of work-in-progress in the accounts of companies in the industry, and the long duration of the work-in-progress stage, make it imperative that accurate costing records are maintained for each job. The costs to be accumulated fall into the usual three categories of direct materials and expenses, direct labour, and overheads. It is very common for substantial parts of the work to be subcontracted, and it is convenient to regard subcontracted work as a separate cost category. A distinction must also be drawn between nominated and other subcontractors.

**4.19** Direct material and expense costs include import duties, transport, handling and other directly attributable costs, less trade discounts, rebates and subsidies. Direct labour input generally involves two categories of personnel, namely permanent skilled employees and employees recruited at each site. Special problems arise in connection with the employment in the UK of casual labour, particularly of the labour only subcontract type, in respect of the need to ensure that all taxes payable and national insurance contributions are correctly levied and accounted for, and these are mentioned in more detail in the auditing section of this chapter.

**4.20** Overheads may conveniently be divided into three main categories:

(a) Those which can be related directly to a specific job;
(b) Those of a central type which can be allocated over a pool of jobs;
(c) Those relating to general activities.

**4.21** An example of (a) is depreciation of plant and machinery such as cranes and bull-dozers. The usual treatment is for depreciation to be calculated on the basis of usage and charged to particular jobs. Where plant is used at different locations it is convenient for a service unit (department or company) to be set up, to which all costs associated with plant (including hired assets) are allocated. A reasonable charge for utilisation of the plant is then made to individual sites and jobs. Those central overheads which can be allocated over a pool of jobs should be included in those job costs by allocation and added to the carrying costs of work-in-progress.

**4.22** Occasionally the cost of a fixed asset used mainly or exclusively for a particular job is charged to the job cost, the asset being revalued (sometimes even upwards) and the revalued balance carried forward at the end of each year. This practice is not to be advocated normally.

**4.23** Each site usually forms a particular cost centre, and the problem common in manufacturing, of allocating shared overheads between a number of different cost centres arises only in the case of those overheads referred to in paragraph 4.20(b).

**4.24** The general overhead category (paragraph 4.20(c)) includes costs of general management, pre-job costs, and interest. These are not normally directly related to particular jobs and should not be included as part of the carrying cost of work-in-progress.

**4.25** Opinions vary as to whether or not interest costs should be written-off or allocated to jobs. It is unusual for such costs to be included in job costs unless sums borrowed are used to finance specific jobs although this is allowed by the Companies Act 1981. In the USA, however, the capitalisation of interest, based on the company's overall interest cost, became mandatory after 15 December 1979. Interest should not be capitalised beyond the date of completion of the relevant project (or part of the project, where it is subdivided into individual parts, as in domestic housing developments).

**4.26** The most significant categories of pre-contract costs are probably the the cost of preparation of feasibility studies, and costs associated with tenders. Such costs are analogous to marketing and are written off as incurred. It is not usual in the UK for costs of successful tenders to be reinstated and charged to the costs of the relevant project although the practice is sometimes encountered in the USA.

**Valuation of work carried out**

**4.27** The preceding section dealt with the elements making up the cost of work-in-progress. The year-end accounts should state work-in-progress in accordance with the requirements of SSAP 9, but the requirements of the Companies Act 1981, particularly Schedule 1 (Sch. 1), are also relevant.

**4.28** SSAP 9 makes a distinction between a short- and long-term contract.

SSAP 9 defines a long-term contract as 'a contract entered into for manufacture or building of a single substantial entity or the provision of a service where the time taken to manufacture, build or provide is such that a substantial proportion of all such contract work will extend for a period exceeding one year'. It requires that contract work-in-progress which falls within that definition should be stated in accounts at 'cost plus any attributable profit, less any forseeable losses, and progress payments received and receivable', (i.e. percentage of completion method).

This is apparently in conflict with the Sch. 1 requirement that stocks (which include work-in-progress) should be included in the balance sheet at the lower of cost and net realisable value. However, although Sch. 1 defines the method of valuation of work-in-progress in the balance sheet, it does not prohibit the recognition of profits. Sch. 1 indicates that profits are to be regarded as realised on the basis of generally accepted accounting principles at the time the accounts are prepared, and the recognition of realised profit on uncompleted long-term contracts is well established and generally accepted, as well as being required by SSAP 9. (See also paragraph 4.65 *et seq.*)

**4.29** SSAP 9 states that all work-in-progress other than long-term contracts should be stated at the lower of cost and net realisable value (i.e. completed contracts method). It should, however, be remembered that the terms 'percentage of completion method' and 'completed contracts method' are not used in SSAP 9.

**4.30** SSAP 9 dictates that the duration of the work, and the nature of the work are the criteria which determine whether or not it should be valued using the completed contracts or percentage of completion method. Difficulties have been encountered in interpreting this definition. The author's view is that contracts of the same type should all be treated in the same way and that it is not correct to make an arbitrary distinction between a contract which takes slightly less than one year to complete and a similar contract which takes slightly more. The apparent rigidity of SSAP 9, based on an arbitrary factor such as the passage of time rather than the nature of the contract involved, does cause controversy. IAS 11 does not place the similar rigid emphasis on the duration of a contract.

**4.31** There are also practical difficulties when considering the concept of a rigid time limit. Normally signature of the contract will determine commencement; however this is not always so and regard should be had to the planned period of the physical work. Even this definition is not clear though, because there will be difficulties with such areas as design, mobilisation, anticipated periods of on-site maintenance, etc. Some would hold that the contract planning before operations commence, and the periods in which the final account/variations/claims are considered, should also be included in the 'year'.

**4.32** Work-in-progress that does not qualify as long-term contract work-in-progress must be valued at the lower of cost and net realisable value, and only in rare circumstances will the inclusion of an element of profit be acceptable. To justify such a departure from the Companies Act and SSAP 9, it would be necessary to show that the recognition of profit only on completion resulted in serious distortions of profits on a regular basis; this circumstance is only likely to arise in very unusual cases.

**Recognition of profit**

**4.33** If a contract falls within the long-term category under SSAP 9, it is necessary to calculate the 'attributable profit' for inclusion in the valuation. Attributable profit is defined as 'that part of the total profit currently estimated to arise over the duration of the contract . . . which fairly reflects the profit attributable to that part of the work performed at the accounting date. (There can be no attributable profit until the outcome of the contract can be assessed with reasonable certainty.)' The sentence in brackets requires emphasis.

**4.34** It is important that prudence should be exercised in estimating both the total anticipated profit on the contract and the proportion thereof attributable to the work completed during the period. SSAP 9 emphasises that many businesses carry out contracts where the outcome cannot reasonably be assessed before conclusion of the contract and in such cases no profit should be taken up.

**4.35** SSAP 9 envisages two situations where no attributable profit can be taken:

(a) Where the contract outcome is not capable of determination in advance because of lack of information, uncertainties, etc.

(b) The earliest point before which profit is not to be taken up has not been reached. This point is determined in the context of the over-riding prudence concept that there can be no attributable profit until the contract's outcome can be foreseen.

**4.36** All foreseeable losses on contracts entered into before the balance-sheet date must be provided in full. (See paragraph 4.48.)

**Calculation of attributable profit**

**4.37** The calculation of attributable profit is not an easy matter. In order to discuss the problems involved, it is necessary to consider the manner under which contracts are priced.

**4.38** Specifications of work may be set out in terms of quantities and values in a document known as the Bill of Quantities (BOQ) at the time a tender is made. A revised version of the BOQ, including details of terms of payment will probably form part of the contract. The contractor will not always price the various stages of a contract to reflect an even incidence of profit; thus for example, the contractor might attribute relatively higher prices to the early stages and relatively lower prices to the later stages in the tendering documents, in order to improve the cash-flow position. This practice is known as 'front-end loading'. The external values attributable to quantities of work carried out will therefore not reflect the overall incidence of profit on the entire contract.

**4.39** The contractor should also prepare, for his internal use, a costing of the projects for which he is tendering. For each stage in a contract, the difference between the internal costing and the pricing in the BOQ will give the profit on that stage. As stated above, the overall profit percentage on the contract may not match the profit percentages in its various stages. The outcome of the various stages of the contract, as they are accomplished, may well be different from budgeted results, and the estimates of costs and revenues to complete the contract will need to be revised during the course of the contract. These realities are recognised in Appendix I to SSAP 9; the explanatory note to which states 'The profit, if any, taken up needs to reflect the proportion of the work carried out at the accounting date, *and to take into account any known inequalities of profitability in the various stages of a contract*'. (Emphasis added.)

**4.40** Inequalities of profitability can arise for several reasons. 'Own work' is generally more profitable than sub-contracted work; 'preliminary' work may, on occasion, even be loss making.

There are two basic approaches to the determination of attributable profit:

(a) The actual profit on the portion of the work completed at the balance sheet date is determined from the priced bill of quantities;

(b) The total anticipated profit is spread over the contract in direct proportion to the work carried out. There are in turn various methods of measuring the work carried out, e.g. by value, by elapsed time, by labour cost or hours.

Either method is acceptable. However, a problem can arise in that tenders are sometimes 'front-end loaded'. This improves the cash flow from the contract, but if the tender prices are used to measure profit, the contract will appear to be very much more profitable in the early stages than it does on completion.

**4.41** The phrase emphasised in 4.39 is compatible with either interpretation. but the effect of employing the two methods is very different. As an example to illustrate this, assume a contractor undertakes the building of a road for £20 million. The project will take three years and the original estimates of total costs are £15 million. Budgeted and actual costs are equal in year 1, but in year 2 labour costs and oil price rises cause a cost over-run, with corresponding effects on costs to complete. The impact of the changed estimate of total costs (£18 million) will be felt particularly on road-building and surfacing costs, and redundancies. All figures are £ million. (*Example overleaf.*)

**4.42** Many contracting companies value their contracts by reference to BOQ prices (method 1) but the whole area is controversial and is one where there is no common ground.

**4.43** Under either method, certain adjustments may be needed to the recorded contract costs for the purposes of calculating attributable profit. Examples of such adjustments are: (a) costs of materials purchased for the contract not yet used, or (b) payments to subcontractors greater or smaller than the amount of work carried out by them. There is always a need for the work of subcontractors to be monitored closely and for any element of prepayment, or underprovision of the actual value of work done in comparison to billings, to be identified and reflected in the accounts. In practice, this is a difficult task, and one which needs careful supervision by senior personnel.

**EXAMPLE**

| *Activity* | | *Costs budgeted initially* | *BOQ as priced* | *Budgeted gross profit* | *Revised schedule of costs* | *Revised gross profit* |
|---|---|---|---|---|---|---|
| Mobilisation costs | Year 1 | 1.5 | 1.9 | 0.4 | 1.5 | 0.4 |
| Earth moving | | 3.5 | 5.0 | 1.5 | 3.5 | 1.5 |
| | | | | | 5.0 | |
| Earth moving | Year 2 | 3.5 | 5.0 | 1.5 | 3.8 | 1.2 |
| Road building | | 3.0 | 4.0 | 1.0 | 4.0 | — |
| | | | | | 12.8 | |
| Surfacing | Year 3 | 2.0 | 2.5 | 0.5 | 3.2 | (0.7) |
| Marking, signals | | 1.0 | 1.1 | 0.1 | 1.0 | 0.1 |
| Wind down/demobilisation/ redundancies | | 0.5 | 0.5 | — | 1.0 | (0.5) |
| | | 15.0 | 20.0 | 5.0 | 18.0 | 2.0 |

| | *Costs* | **Method 1** *Profit added to costs using BOQ prices* | **Method 2** *Profit added to costs by reference to proportion of work completed* |
|---|---|---|---|
| *At end of year 1* | | | |
| Work completed = | 5.0 | | |
| Gross profit: (0.4 + 1.5) | | 1.9 | |
| Gross profit: $\frac{5}{15} \times 5$ | | | 1.7 |
| Cumulative | 5.0 | 1.9 | 1.7 |
| *At end of year 2* | | | |
| Work completed = | 7.8 | | |
| Gross profit: (1.2 + 0) | | 1.2 | |
| (but reduced to 0.1 because cumulative total profit cannot exceed 2.0) | | (1.1) | |
| | | 0.1 | |
| Gross profit: $\frac{(12.8 \times 2.0)}{18} - 1.7$ | | | (0.3) |
| Cumulative | 12.8 | 2.0 | 1.4 |
| *Year 3* (assuming no further changes) | 5.2 | (Nil) | 0.6 |
| | 18.0 | 2.0 | 2.0 |

**4.44** In any individual job there may be several indicators of the physical progress and the most appropriate one must be determined in the light of the particular circumstances. For example, a comparison of cost of work to date and estimated total cost is usually the most appropriate in the case of a building project, whereas in the case of a contract to build a pipeline, a comparison of completed and total length may be more appropriate.

**4.45** In order to ensure close adherence to the concept of prudence, the portion of work on which profit is taken under the percentage of completion method may be limited to the portion of work inspected and accepted by the contract owner's representative.

**4.46** As discussed earlier, SSAP 9 requires the completed contracts method to be adopted for long-term contracts only when their outcome is not capable of determination in advance. In such circumstances profit is recognised when the relevant project is substantially complete. Bearing in mind the uncertainties which must have been deemed to surround the outcome of the contract, the determination of the relevant cut-off point is not without difficulty. Appendix 2 to SSAP 9 gives the following guidance on the matter of when a long-term contract is complete; when '. . . no further work, apart from maintenance work, is expected to take place'. The AICPA Accounting Research Bulletin No. 45 considers this problem and states that a contract is substantially complete when remaining costs are not anticipated to be significant in amount.

**4.47** The legal framework within which particular projects are carried out is also relevant. For example, in the case of speculative domestic housing, it would be reasonable to recognise profits on exchange of contracts for sale of the houses. It would be imprudent to recognise profits at the time of offer, and it might be over-prudent to wait until completion had taken place.

**Provisions against loss-making contracts**

**4.48** SSAP 9 requires that all foreseeable losses on contracts be provided in full (whether profit is being recognised under the 'completed contract' or the 'percentage of completion' method). Provision for anticipated losses should be made irrespective of:

(a) Whether or not work has commenced on such contracts;

(b) The proportion of work carried out to date;

(c) The amount of profit expected to arise on other contracts.

In practice, inter-related contracts relating to a particular project with the same client are often taken together when determining the necessity of provision for losses. In the early stages, provisions necessary on a contract may exceed the value of work carried out; in such cases, the provision should be deducted from the value (on a contract by contract basis) and the excess should be shown in current liabilities.

### The project review

**4.49** The fact that costs are accumulated over a considerable period of time necessitates close monitoring of the comparison of costs with budgets and both of these with projected income. Such reviews will be an important procedure for management and for auditors.

**4.50** A major accounting problem with construction work lies in ensuring that all costs to date have been recorded. It is important that progress on all subcontracted work be closely monitored so that adequate amounts may be accrued at each accounting date; such reviews will have to take account of claims by subcontractors and cost increases which they may be able to claim under the terms of relevant agreements.

**4.51** The impact of inflation will be considerable and requires careful attention in compiling costs to complete. The terms of the main contract will usually determine the effect of inflation on the contractor. Certain types of contract, known variously as 'cost reimbursement plus fee', 'management contracts', 'cost plus fixed fee' etc., effectively place the burden of inflationary cost increases on the client, although such contracts often contain rigorous exclusions as to cost increases due to contractors' inefficiency. Certain 'fixed price' contracts also have 'fluctuation' or 'escalation' clauses, which effectively regulate the apportionment between the parties of cost increases due to inflation, by reference to agreed indices. All these aspects must be covered in the contract review.

**4.52** In carrying out the periodic reviews, attention needs to be paid to losses arising on major contracts which would be expected to absorb a considerable part of the general and administrative overheads of the contractor in future years. In such cases, the relevant administration and general overheads of future years should be included in the loss provision. Any obligation of the contractor for rectification, maintenance or guarantee work must also be carefully considered.

**4.53** One factor which can cause a substantial change in the expected outcome of a project is the fluctuation in foreign exchange rates on overseas jobs. Whilst most companies would wish to remove all exchange risks from their jobs, the need to present competitive tenders usually prevents them from doing so. Exchange fluctuations on a major job drawn up with, say, a five per cent profit margin, can affect the entire existence of a company, and not just the outcome and the job concerned. Construction companies have adopted a variety of methods to shield themselves against exchange fluctuations, including the taking of loans in foreign currency to balance their exchange exposure, and participation in the ECGD 'tender to contract scheme'. It is usual to charge the cost of hedging currency receivable as part of job costs, in the same way as insurance costs are so charged. Known foreign-exchange losses on unhedged portions of projects will need to be provided as part of loss provisions.

**4.54** It is common for variations to be made to the original terms of the contract during its course at the request of the client. When a significant variation to a contract is agreed in principle, but the value thereof has not been settled, a conservative estimate of the value should be included in the calculation of the total sales value of the contract. In determining the overall value of contract, dayworks should also be valued on a conservative basis, but with particular regard to their recoverability.

**4.55** Changes in circumstances surrounding a project often give rise to claims by the contractor against the client. Claims should not be included in the estimates of total income from a contract until they have been agreed. In practice, agreement of most claims extends beyond the completion of the work. The guidance given in SSAP 9 Appendix I is based on the view that the potentially distorting effects on profit and loss accounts of later periods of the incidence of successful claims is preferable to anticipating additional revenue which may not, in fact, materialise or which may be revised downwards from its original estimate.

**4.56** Pending agreement of claims, the possibility of the existence of counter-claims from the owner and of related claims against the contractor by his subcontractor, should be borne in mind. If necessary, a provision should be made in the accounts, or a summary of the situation may have to be disclosed as a note on contingencies if the amount involved is material.

**Disclosure in accounts**

**4.57** The disclosure requirements are governed by the Companies Acts and by SSAP 9. Three of the statutory requirements laid down in the Companies Acts are worth specific mention. (See paragraphs 4.58, 4.61 and 4.65 below.)

**4.58** There is the requirement to disclose the amount and basis of computing turnover (defined in paragraph 94, Sch. 1). Turnover in the construction industry is not such a readily understandable figure as that in manufacturing. In the case of work which is accounted for under the completed-contracts method, all the contract value will be included as turnover at the point at which a contract is complete. In the case of contracts accounted for under the percentage of completion method, the turnover figure should give the reader of the accounts an indication of the level of activity carried out. This aim will usually be achieved by taking turnover to be the gross value of contract work carried out in the period.

**4.59** The need to revise previous estimates (of profit included in work in progress) in the light of changed circumstances when arriving at the current year's attributable profit may result in the profit to turnover ratio fluctuating widely from year to year. It is a requirement for material factors causing distortions to the normal trend to be disclosed in order to show the 'true and fair' view.

**4.60** The question of whether or not reimbursable costs incurred on a contract should be included in the computation of turnover also requires attention. It is important that each case be decided on its merits. There are certain contracts, such as 'procurement contracts', where the contractor is merely acting as agent for the contract owner and the reimbursable costs should not be classified as turnover. However, where a contractor acts as contract manager on a particular project it would seem preferable to include the fee and reimbursable costs as turnover to give an indication of the amount of activity in the year.

**4.61** The manner in which work in progress has been computed must be disclosed. This requirement will be relevant to most construction companies and in the case of long-term contracts, SSAP 9 recommends as a description 'cost plus attributable profit (if any), less foreseeable losses (if any), and progress payments received and receivable'.

**4.62** A retention (usually calculated as a percentage of the amount certified for payment) will normally be deducted from payments made to the contractor pending satisfactory completion of part or all of the contract. It is common for retentions not to be treated as debtors by the contractor, and hence deducted from work-in-progress.

**4.63** In the case of 'front end loaded contracts' total receipts in the early stages of contracts (less retentions) may well exceed the adjusted value of work carried out. Payments received in excess of this adjusted value of work carried out to date (on a contract by contract basis) should be shown as current liabilities and disclosed separately if material.

**4.64** The deduction of progress payments from contract work-in-progress has the effect of reducing the net figure for work-in-progress stated in the balance sheet, and hence the apparent significance of the contract to the reader of the accounts. SSAP 9 requires the elements making up the net valuation of the contracts to be disclosed by way of note. IAS 11 requires a further analysis of the gross figure for contract work-in-progress between amounts valued on the percentage of completion and amounts valued on the completed contract method.

**4.65** The Companies Act 1981 Schedule 1 requirement (now paragraph 22 of Schedule 8 of the Companies Act 1948) is that 'the amount to be included in respect of any current asset shall be its purchase price or production cost'. This is in obvious conflict with the SSAP 9 requirement already mentioned relating to long-term contract work-in-progress. There would appear to be several presentations which would comply with the various requirements, but directors will have to determine whether, in order to present a 'true and fair view', it is necessary to invoke the 'over-ride' provided for in the 'new' Section 149 of the Companies Act 1948, sub-sections 3 and 4. Where the directors of a company depart from the legislative requirements then particulars of that departure, the reason for it and its effect, must be given in a note to the accounts.

**4.66** The first alternative is to include work-in-progress at cost and payments on account received in the overall heading of 'stocks' and the profit element which has been recognised in 'prepayments and accrued income'. This approach would be suitable where the ownership of the work has not yet passed to the buyer, and where profit is being taken on part of the work which has not been the subject of a payment on account.

**4.67** The second alternative is to exclude from work-in-progress the cost of that part of the contract which has been billed to the client, and similarly to exclude the payments on account received. Any retentions on the amounts billed, or any payments on account receivable, but unpaid, would then be included in debtors. This presentation would be appropriate where the ownership of the work completed passed immediately to the buyer and he was billed at regular intervals for the work as it was completed. This is the position with most construction and civil engineering contracts. In effect, the amounts billed to the buyer are treated as sales rather than as payments on account of uncompleted contracts. This treatment could have financial disadvantages.

**4.68** Strictly speaking, neither of the above alternative presentations complies with SSAP 9 and in order to meet the intention of that Standard it will also be necessary to disclose:

(a) The amount of work-in-progress at cost, plus attributable profit, less foreseeable losses; and

(b) Cash received and receivable at the accounting date as progress payments on account of contracts in progress.

**4.69** The disclosure of this information, along with the different information required to comply with the Companies Act, seems likely to result in accounts becoming confusing. There is now (August 1983) considerable debate within the construction industry concerning the detailed way in which a departure from the legislation should be shown. The debate concerns, *inter alia*, whether the amount of profit so included in the work-in-progress needs to be disclosed as being the 'effect' of a departure from the Companies Act. The view which gives the maximum disclosure might result in the undermentioned detail:

**EXAMPLE**

| | *1983* | *1982* |
|---|---|---|
| *Stocks* | *£'000* | *£'000* |
| Raw materials and consumables | 704 | 599 |
| Work-in-progress | | |
| At cost | 3,074 | 2,238 |
| Provision for future losses | (650) | — |
| Attributable profit on long-term contracts | 192 | 441 |
| | 2,616 | 2,679 |
| Payments on account | (1,856) | (2,110) |
| Net work-in-progress | 760 | 569 |
| Balance sheet total | 1,464 | 1,168 |

Wording to accompany this example might be:

'The inclusion of attributable profit in long-term contract work-in-progress in accordance with SSAP 9 constitutes a departure from the statutory valuation rules and is required by Section 149 (3) of the Companies Act 1948 to enable the accounts to give a true and fair view. The amount of attributable profit is on work completed to date and is disclosed above.'

**4.70** An alternative view being advocated, and which is likely to be followed by many, suggests that it is only necessary to disclose the amount of profit in the net balance-sheet work-in-progress (i.e. after deducting payments on account). Those who support this view also argue that since payments on account are not divided between 'cost' and 'profit' then it would be impracticable to ascertain how much profit is included in the net work-in-progress and so any allocation between the two would be artificial and the resulting figure would not be meaningful. Such a figure might also be immaterial. Thus, a more probable, though less useful disclosure, might be as under:

**EXAMPLE**

| | 1983 | 1982 |
|---|---|---|
| *Stocks* | *£'000* | *£'000* |
| Raw materials and consumables | 704 | 599 |
| Long-term contract work-in-progress | | |
| Costs to date plus attributable profit less provision for losses | 2,616 | 2,679 |
| Less: Payments on account | (1,856) | (2,110) |
| Net work-in-progress | 760 | 569 |
| Balance sheet total | 1,464 | 1,168 |

Wording which might accompany the above example might be:

'The inclusion of attributable profit in long-term work-in-progress in accordance with SSAP 9 constitutes a departure from the statutory valuation rules and is required by Section 149 (3) of the Companies Act 1948 to enable the accounts to give a true and fair view. As progress payments cannot meaningfully be allocated between cost and profit it is impracticable to quantify the effect of the departure on the amount of long-term contract work-in-progress included in the balance sheet.'

**4.71** The Accounting Standards Committee (ASC) has considered the conflict and whilst concluding that SSAP 9 should remain in force without amendment, issued a statement on 1 August 1983 that it has a policy of not issuing interpretations. However, the ASC has also indicated that any company concerned with the conflict should be encouraged to obtain its own legal advice.

The directors of each company are therefore left to consider the conflict in the light of its own circumstances and arrive at the appropriate conclusion having taken any relevant advice.

**Current cost accounting (CCA)**

**4.72** The discussions above have been in the context of historical cost accounts. The current cost data requiring disclosure under SSAP 16 takes the historical cost information as a starting point, and the foregoing discussions will therefore also be relevant in the context of CCA. Certain additional considerations arise, however, when CCA principles are applied to the construction industry, and these derive from the special features of the industry.

**4.73** In the case of contracts, it is usual for payments on account to be made as work progresses. When cash is received by a contractor for work done, his investment in that work-in-progress will be liquidated and he will be able to apply the funds thus released to other work. Therefore, although he must provide for cost increases relating to the work before a payment is received, he will not need to make provision beyond the date of receipt of funds. The cost of sales adjustment (COSA) should therefore be calculated by reference to work-in-progress as reduced by payments received on account.

**4.74** Where different rates of price change affect different elements of cost, it will be necessary to allocate payments received over the different elements. Unless there are special considerations which make another allocation appropriate, it is reasonable to do this on a pro-rata basis. If payments received on account of any single contract exceed the cost of the work done then the excess should be treated as borrowings and dealt with through the gearing adjustment.

**4.75** Where businesses carry out unique contracts, it may well be that there is no relevant measure of replacement cost available, since any subsequent contract is likely to be significantly different in nature and incidence of cost. In such cases it is appropriate to treat work-in-progress as a monetary asset. This has two effects:

(a) The COSA is effectively treated as part of the monetary working capital adjustment (MWCA);

(b) Work-in-progress appears in the CCA balance sheet at the same amount as in the historical cost balance sheet rather than at replacement cost.

It is usually desirable for all contract work-in-progress to be treated in the same way; it is likely to be confusing if some work is subject to a COSA, while other work is treated as monetary working capital.

**4.76** Because it will normally be treated as a monetary item, CCA will have no effect on the valuation of work-in-progress in the balance sheet, although the profit and loss account will be affected by the MWCA.

## United Kingdom taxation

**4.77** UK taxation law does not define 'profits', but the Inland Revenue usually accept taxable profits to be the surplus which would be recognised on the basis of reasonable accounting conventions, subject to specified adjustments. Normally this causes little concern and audited accounts are accepted as the basis from which liabilities are computed.

**4.78** Prior to the introduction of SSAP 9, companies following the completed contract method of accounting had recognised profits in the year of completion of the contract for accounts and tax purposes and no timing differences arose. After the introduction of SSAP 9, tax would normally be levied on the profits recognised in valuing work-in-progress on the percentage of completion method. The profit recognised would be after providing in full for all foreseeable losses. The Inland Revenue, in a statement of practice, stated that they would only allow provisions for losses on contracts to be set off to the extent that they related to work carried out to the end of the accounting period. A timing difference would therefore arise relating to the difference between allowable losses and those anticipated losses fully taken into account for accounting purposes, since the latter would relate to the entirety of the period of the contract.

**4.79** Under the rules relating to stock appreciation relief, contained in the Finance Act 1981, relief is given on the basis of a percentage increase (calculated according to published indices) on the value of opening stocks and work-in-progress after deducting payments on account. An architect's certificate of 'practical completion' is usually issued when work on a contract is substantially complete; this is followed in due course by a 'final certificate'. Work-in-progress usually continues to be eligible for stock appreciation relief until the final certificate is issued.

**4.80** Stock which has been invoiced as sold is usually not eligible for stock relief. In contracting work, interim applications are made which are not invoices. The client or his agent will take the application, allow parts and disallow others. Only the net amount will be certified and paid in the form of progress payments. The amounts payable according to such certificates are nonetheless eligible for relief until they have been settled.

**4.81** Under SSAP 15, deferred taxation should be provided in respect of the tax effects of all timing differences other than those which can be demonstrated with reasonable probability to continue in the foreseeable future (defined as three years). Under the 1981 stock relief rules, the relief given will not normally be 'clawed back' unless there has been a significant reduction in trading activity. It is therefore unlikely that, under normal circumstances, a deferred tax provision would be required in respect of stock appreciation relief. However, because joint-venture companies are common in the construction industry, it may be necessary to consider clawback of stock relief in a different light where such a company has a finite life, (e.g. the construction of a 'one-off' project). As there is thus the certainty of clawback deferred taxation should be provided.

**4.82** Development Land Tax (DLT), which came into force in 1976, is charged on the increase in the value of land due to a change in its use, for example, from agricultural to residential use. Increases in the existing use value of land are not chargeable to DLT. Thus an increase in the value during the development stage of land bought with planning permission is not chargeable to DLT.

**4.83** DLT is not a tax on profits (which are taxed after being earned) and becomes chargeable on the commencement of a development, although there are certain provisions for deferral of its payment. Where DLT arises as a result of disposal, the liability should be charged against the consideration received. Where DLT arises other than on disposal (as on commencement of development) it should, for accounts purposes, be included in the carrying value of the project, even if the actual payment of the liability is deferred.

### Auditing considerations

**4.84** All industries have their own auditing considerations. In the case of the construction industry the one consideration more vital than any to the auditor is knowledge of his client's business, history and philosophy. The author would go so far as to say that in few other industries is there the requirement to exercise such a degree of judgement as in the audit of a constructor for, as is recognised in SSAP 9, the valuation of work-in-progress is largely based on opinions and is by no means a precise science. Unless the auditor has great confidence in his client he has serious problems in ensuring that work-in-progress has been properly reviewed and valued correctly. Apart from this area it is not thought that auditing considerations associated with the construction industry are any more acute than those found in other industries, although they are different in kind.

**4.85** An auditor is always concerned with evidence which will support (or refute) the truth and fairness of figures in accounts. The auditor of a construction client very often finds he cannot rely on direct evidence to support the work-in-progress valuation. Since the valuation itself is often largely arrived at as a result of future cost and income projections, the audit approach must also be judgemental.

**4.86** The auditor has to accumulate a variety of indirect evidence regarding the reasonableness of his client's valuation of work-in-progress. In doing so he must begin by obtaining complete familiarity with all aspects of his client's business. He then has to consider a series of questions bearing on the valuation in the light of his knowledge of the client, the business and the job involved. It is not possible in the following paragraphs to do more than indicate some of the questions which need to be considered by the auditor.

**4.87** Tendering for contracts:

(a) Has the prevailing economic climate affected the client's tendering procedures?

(b) Is a down-turn in business forcing the client to cut his margins 'to the bone', thus increasing the likelihood of a contract becoming unprofitable?

(c) Is rapid expansion or keen competition forcing the client to undertake contracts where he does not have previous experience – if so, how reliable will be the client's own estimations?

(d) Is the client maintaining strict procedures to 'vet' the credit worthiness of the parties inviting tenders?

**4.88** Bill of quantities/internal costings:

(a) How reliable is the client's system for costing and for devising billing schedules to meet cash-flow needs?

(b) Are anticipated changes in labour and overhead charges reasonable?

(c) Are the potential penalties for delays in completion built into the costing?

(d) Are costs of rectification properly covered?

(e) Does the client's system ensure that physical progress on jobs is quantified at regular intervals?

**4.89** Contract review:

(a) Does management obtain timely reports as to changes from planned progress?

(b) Are the full financial implications of variations for changed circumstances costed and their effect on the contract's final outcome quantified?

(c) Have the terms of changes to the contract been accepted in writing by the employer? Are approved variations distinguished from changes caused by disruptions and other unapproved factors?

(d) How closely does management monitor progress on claims by and claims against them?

(e) How closely have original and revised schedules and budgets been met in the past?

(f) Is the client encountering any technical or engineering difficulties which might delay completion of the contract?

(g) How reasonable is the client's method for profit recognition?

(h) What is the philosophy regarding foreseeable losses?

(i) What is the track record? Have there been any management changes or policy changes which might affect this?

**4.90** Throughout the duration of a contract the auditor should place only limited audit reliance on amounts certified for payment. Amounts accepted at any one time may subsequently be challenged and usually only at final account stage do they become absolutely certain. This applies to the contract with the employer and also to the contractor's position with sub-contractors.

**4.91** The recruitment of site labour can cause audit difficulties in relation to the completeness of site costs. It is much more difficult to verify the completeness and accuracy of the labour charges associated with non-permanent employees than is the case with a permanent labour force. The auditor's main concern arises from the need to ensure that all labour costs have been accounted for, including, for example, payroll related expenses such as National Insurance, or accident costs, and that they are accounted for in the correct period. He will have to rely to a large extent on his client's control mechanisms, such as adequate site supervision, internal reports and accountability of site controllers.

**4.92** A good example of the need for control mechanisms results from the Construction Industry Tax Deduction Scheme for making payments to subcontractors. The auditor has to satisfy himself that adequate procedures have been set up and carried out on site and at head office in relation to the checking of the validity of exemption certificates.

**4.93** The application of the concept of materiality to the accounts of construction companies is not without difficulty. One of the auditor's main concerns is to ascertain whether or not accounts give a true and fair view, without material mis-statement. Materiality is usually determined by reference to the year's income statement since the net profit figure is usually the most important figure for readers of accounts. A problem in the construction industry is that a figure which is a relatively small percentage of work-in-progress can have a totally disproportionate impact on profits. One such significant factor which may affect the net profit figure results from a restatement or revision of the value of work-in-progress (such as revised estimates of costs to complete or gross income) and provisions for contract losses. These areas require particular care by the auditor.

**4.94** One final important part of the audit process is to ensure adequate audit site attendance visits – particularly to remote or overseas contracts. In this way first-hand evidence is obtained of actual conditions which can often usefully be backed up by photographs taken by the auditor. Discussion on site with site officials will often reveal problem areas which might not otherwise be apparent.

**4.95** It will be appreciated that by far the hardest task of the auditor of a client in the construction industry is to examine the reasonableness of his client's periodic evaluation of costs to completion in the light of existing and expected circumstances. This examination of future events is not one usually associated with financial reporting. The auditor is given some comfort by his post-balance-sheet review of the events affecting the year-end figures. By the time his opinion on year-end accounts is formulated, at least two or three months will usually have elapsed from the year-end, and general events (such as the state of the economy) and specific events (such as the receipt of notice of claims, variation orders or even construction failure), may affect the view taken by management and the auditor on the likely outcome of jobs. The importance of the auditor's consideration of this area must be viewed in the context of the business environment in which many constructors operate, namely small margins and considerable exposure to possible loss of working capital.

# FARMING

E. M. W. Robson

## Background to the business

**5.01** The total area farmed in the UK is now around 19 million hectares, of which seven million hectares constitutes arable farmland. Farming has developed from a labour-intensive industry with many small farms to a highly mechanised business on much larger farms. The actual number of farm holdings in the UK decreased from 445,000 in 1964 to 249,000 in 1979. Farming encompasses a great range of activities varying from sheep and beef production in the hill and upland areas of Scotland, the north of England and Wales to the many varieties of arable farming in the rich flat arable areas of Scotland and England. Within the constraints of a chapter it is not possible to cover all types of arable and livestock farming, so to illustrate the problems of stock valuation, this chapter concentrates on arable (cereals and potatoes) and livestock (cattle) operations. Many of the criteria which follow apply equally well to all forms of arable farming and husbandry. It is essential for the auditor to understand the type of farming being carried out.

**5.02** Farming stocks can generally be divided into:

(a) arable stocks;

(b) livestock (cattle);

(c) stores on farms.

## Arable stocks

**5.03** The crop cycle has three principal valuation elements:

(a) *Tillages*. The preparation of the land for planting. This includes such operations as ploughing, rolling, fertilizer spreading and harrowing ready for the next stage of drilling. The costs involved are labour and machinery costs.

(b) *In-ground valuation (work-in-progress).* Drilling or planting and thereafter applying fertilizers and sprays to encourage growth and to control weeds and disease. The costs are the purchase price of seeds, fertilizers and sprays, and the labour and machinery costs involved in their application.

(c) *Harvested crop valuation.* In the case of wheat and barley the crop is harvested, dried, and put into store. In the case of potatoes the crop is harvested, sorted, graded and put into store. The main costs involved in harvesting are the labour and machinery costs. In the case of potatoes, harvesting normally includes a large proportion of casual labour.

**Livestock (cattle)**

**5.04** This stock can be divided into two categories:

(a) *Beef-production cattle.* These are reared principally to produce calves for finishing for beef. These cattle usually suckle their calves to six months of age. After weaning, the cattle may then be sold as stores or finished on grass or concentrates.

(b) *Dairy-production cattle.* These are reared principally for milk production, although calves are an important by-product. Calves surplus to herd requirements can be sold or finished on the farm for beef or sold after 2–2½ years as down-calving heifers. It is not therefore always possible to isolate dairy-production cattle as a separate category completely distinct from beef production. Production cattle are further subdivided for stock purposes into young stock and mature livestock. From the time a calf is born it takes between 2–2½ years, in the case of a heifer, before it is ready to be transferred to the production herd, and 18 months in the case of a young bull, before it is ready for breeding purposes.

**Stores on farms**

**5.05** This category will include items such as seeds, fertilisers, sprays, feedstuffs, machinery, spares and fuel at their bought-in cost, and silage, hay and straw at cost.

**Other business considerations**

**5.06** The farming industry is subject to a considerable degree of government control. Agricultural wage rates are fixed annually by the Agricultural Wages Board. Farm products themselves are subject to different marketing arrangements. For example, the operation of the Milk Marketing Board in the UK is an integral part of price support under the Common Agricultural Policy (CAP) since there are intervention prices operating in the case of milk products which underpin the national support measures which themselves dictate the price paid to the producer. In the case of potatoes, which have only recently come within the European Economic Community (EEC) regime a price guarantee operates, but as this is only a guarantee to the market, it is possible for the producer to sell at well below the guarantee price. Similar measures operate for sheep. Some farm products are outside any EEC or national support mechanism, for example, poultry products. Success in cereal farming (i.e. a high tonnage per hectare) is significantly affected by weather conditions. The price per tonne is also influenced by world-market prices and by the quantity of the product itself. For example milling wheat commands a higher price than feed wheat as does malting barley over feed barley. Under the CAP the operation of the reference rate or green pound, the mechanism by which EEC prices are converted into pounds sterling, underpins the UK support arrangements for particular commodities.

**Accounting/auditing problems**

*Physical existence and ownership*

**5.07** In the case of cattle it is usual for large farms to use the services of an independent valuer or agent to count and categorise cattle. On the other hand if the farmer undertakes his own stock count, the auditor should attend at the time of the count to confirm the numbers. These counts taken in conjunction with a reconciliation of numbers from beginning to end of the year should significantly contribute to confirming cattle numbers.

**5.08** If, however, the herd or part of the herd has been sent elsewhere for grazing it is important to establish whether or not ownership vests with the farm being audited. It is important to review the nature of the agreement to establish whether the ownership remains with the farmer, subject to payment of grazing rent or 'agistment', or whether the cattle are actually sold and repurchased at a margin equivalent to the grazing rent.

**5.09** In the case of dairy cattle, in particular pedigree herds, detailed records for each animal are usually kept and these can be tested to ensure that the cattle have been properly classified.

**5.10** It is also usual for large arable farms to use the services of the professional valuer. The valuer arrives at a value for crops knowing what has been planted or drilled, determining seed and fertilizer application and adding charge rates for work done. Some large farms maintain detailed crop records and operate a proper costing system. These records further help the auditor to establish the existence of the tillages and the in-ground valuation.

**5.11** Stores on farms too are often counted by the independent professional valuer. They should also be readily available for inspection at the year-end. It should be noted that agricultural merchants often hold stocks of fertilizers and sprays which belong to the farm. Major suppliers should be asked to supply written confirmation of details of stocks held by them.

**5.12** At the year-end the auditor will need to identify and ensure a proper cut-off point between the stages of production. In particular the transfer of seeds, sprays and fertilizers from stores to 'work-in-progress' should be subjected to 'cut-off' tests.

*Production costs*

**5.13** As discussed earlier, arable stock and 'work-in-progress' is divided into three chronologically distinct areas for stock valuation – tillages and in-ground valuation forming the work in progress, harvested crop valuation being the finished goods. Costs incurred must therefore be properly charged to each stage of production.

**5.14** The costing system will generally charge individual crops with those costs specifically relating to that crop (e.g. seeds, fertilizers and sprays) and will treat other costs (e.g. machinery and labour costs) as fixed costs which are not allocated. At the year-end these general costs should be apportioned, on a reasonable basis, to work-in-progress and finished goods. Unless detailed allocations are maintained, it is usually necessary to use external sources for information on the cost of the various operations performed. Examples of such sources are the National Association of Agricultural Contractors and Wye College. When using such sources, the auditor should ensure that these guide prices are suitably adjusted to reflect individual circumstances, for example downward adjustments for economies of scale. By referring to these sources the auditor can confirm that independent professional valuations are reasonable.

To summarise, the auditor needs to satisfy himself that:

(a) Specific costs are correctly identified and allocated;

(b) A suitable basis is used to apportion general costs; and

(c) Costs per hectare look reasonable compared with previous years.

**5.15** As with arable stocks, the two problems involved in livestock valuation, are the assessment of costs and the correct allocation between 'work-in-progress' and 'finished goods'.

**5.16** Work-in-progress is represented by immature heifers and young bulls. Finished goods consist of mature livestock, i.e. the production beef or dairy herds and stock bulls. In the case of cattle, costs are incurred from birth until sale or death, but revenue is not earned until they 'mature'. Dairy heifers mature when they have calved and are in milk production; young bulls mature when they are ready for breeding purposes.

**5.17** Consequently, the distinction between immature and mature livestock is important. Until livestock are sufficiently mature to earn revenue, costs incurred should not be charged to the profit and loss account but should be accumulated in stock. On maturity this treatment is reversed and all subsequent costs will be charged to the profit and loss account as incurred to be matched with the revenue earned in milk production and sale of calves.

**5.18** Attention should be paid to establishing the costs incurred and the distinction between immature and mature livestock.

**5.19** The costs incurred will mainly comprise feedstuffs and grazing. Feedstuffs will usually represent a charge from stocks on farm or harvested crops, for example silage, concentrates, feed barley etc. Grazing will be the cost of grass crops grown (i.e. a charge from arable stocks) or the agistment or grazing charge.

**5.20** To distinguish between immature and mature livestock, the auditor should ensure that adequate livestock records are maintained. These records should show the date of birth of each heifer and bull, together with milk production, calving and breeding records. These records can also help him form a view of the net-realisable value.

**5.21** In the case of beef cattle, there is usually no specific attempt made in practice to allocate costs of mature and immature livestock separately, as all charges go to the profit and loss account and any difference in treatment is reflected in the year-end valuation.

### Net-realisable value

*Arable stocks*

**5.22** Most farmers farm with a view to profit and therefore the net-realisable value of their stocks should normally be greater than cost. Tillages represent preparation of the land for the following season's in-ground valuation, i.e. the tillage cost plus the cost of applying seeds, fertilizers and sprays. Harvested crops represent the in-ground valuation plus the cost of harvesting, drying and storing. There are daily-quoted prices available for wheat, barley etc. and the auditor should compare these with the prices used to ensure that the net-realisable value is greater than cost. Any after-date sales should also provide comfort to the auditor, both as to realisable value and, if a considerable part of the harvest has been sold after date, as to tonnage. The auditor should ensure that the storage facilities are good and, if not, check the grain as to its condition. For tillages and in-ground valuation, it is useful to compare previous years' costs with the current year and obtain explanations for the variation, for example, rise in cost of diesel fuel, increase in wage rates etc. An analytical review of the results of the farm is an essential part of the audit.

*Livestock (cattle)*

**5.23** The majority of livestock farms do not maintain detailed costing records and depend therefore on a professional valuation of the market value at the end of the financial period. The Inland Revenue recognise that some effort is necessary to bring the herd to a market condition and allow 60 per cent of this figure as an acceptable basis for the cost of the herd. The auditor should confirm whether the professional valuation has taken this matter into consideration.

**5.24** On the other hand, many dairy farmers do maintain cost of production records for their replacements to the milking herd, i.e. the cost of growing a calf into a 2–2½ year old down calved heifer. Once included in the herd at this cost, all further costs relate directly to the production of milk and calves.

**5.25** To ensure that the valuation is reasonable, the auditor can compare the figures used in it with market prices obtainable for like animals at the local market, discounted by 40 per cent, at the financial period end.

**Taxation considerations**

**5.26** Valuations made for accounting purposes which accord with SSAP 9 will hold good for taxation purposes.

**5.27** Farming stocks generally qualify as trading stock for the purposes of stock relief. Occasionally some difficulties occur in relation to consumable stores not directly related to production as, for example, fuel oil for haulage of production.

**5.28** Although not strictly concerned with the matter of valuation, an important element of the taxation treatment of production herds is the right of election for the herd basis.

**5.29** In general terms, a production herd is treated as a capital asset so that the cost of creating the herd may not be deducted in calculating taxable profits and it follows that the proceeds of the sale of that asset are not taxable as trading receipts nor are they chargeable as capital gains.

**5.30** The net cost of replacement of an animal in the herd is allowed as a trading expense. There will thus be an addition to profits representing the proceeds of sale of the animal replaced and a charge against profit for the cost of the new animal, i.e. a reduction of stock. Where an animal is merely added to the herd from trading stock, there will be an addition to profit of the cost of rearing the animal. In the case of an animal bred by the farmer, the cost is usually taken to be 75 per cent (for pigs and sheep), 60 per cent (for cattle) or the market value at the time, although the exact figure is a matter for agreement with the Inland Revenue and, in the case of other animals this will be necessary in any event.

**5.31** There are detailed provisions to deal with additions to and reductions from the herd as well as provisions concerning compulsory slaughter.

**5.32** The election for the herd basis must be made as regards all production herds of a particular class and is irrevocable.

**5.33** For a detailed appreciation of the taxation of farms and woodlands there is a Chartac Taxation Guide by Camamile, Davison and Sarson published by the Institute of Chartered Accountants in England and Wales (2nd edition, 1982).

# HOTELS

## C. R. Plummer

### Background to the business

**6.01** A large proportion of a hotel's costs are fixed and do not vary with the number of guests or customers that make use of its facilities. Also a hotel cannot recoup revenue it loses through unlet rooms, and food and (to a lesser extent) beverages are perishable products. Consequently, a hotel's profitability is highly sensitive to changes in demand that may be outside the management's control.

**6.02** Individual transactions within a hotel are typically for small money amounts, and both guests and outsiders will be paying for a variety of services either in cash or on credit. This means that a number of employees both collect cash and record charges in different places. As a result, good internal control over cash receipts and debtors is essential. However, the principles that should apply to purchasing, storing and issuing stocks are similar to those that are applied in other businesses.

### The materiality of stocks

**6.03** Where the reporting entity owns the hotel property, the balance-sheet value of stocks may be insignificant in relation to the entity's total assets. The value of stocks is also low in relation to sales income, because food stocks are typically turned over between 20 and 40 times per annum, and beverage stocks are typically turned over between seven and eight times per annum.

### Classification of stocks

**6.04** Hotel stocks can conveniently be classified both by type and storage location in the following way:

(a) Food (perishable and non-perishable):

  (i) In dry goods stores (non-perishable foods).

  (ii) In the kitchen(s), including day-to-day supplies of frozen foods.

  (iii) In bulk freezers, particularly in large hotels where substantial stores of food, especially meat, are held.

(b) Beverages (wines, spirits, soft drinks, and tobacco):
   (i) In bars and dispenser bars.
   (ii) In wine cellars or beverage stores.
   (iii) In bonded stores, particularly for larger hotels.
   (iv) In the custody of the supplier either in the United Kingdom, or, overseas, until required.

(c) Linen, silverware, china and glass in the appropriate reserve store.

(d) Maintenance and general stores (including cleaning materials, stationery, guest supplies, and small equipment):
   (i) In the maintenance store;
   (ii) In the dry goods store(s).

In smaller hotels, some of the above storage locations will not be physically separate from others.

**The accounting treatment of stocks**

*Food*

**6.05** Non-perishable foods consist of numerous, low-value items. Issues from the stores are made frequently and to many cost centres. Detailed stock records are not usually maintained, so that issues cannot be valued on a first-in, first-out basis. Consequently, issues are typically valued at the latest available invoice price of the goods.

**6.06** Perishable and frozen foods are often delivered directly to the kitchens, where the chef should control all issues. Because all foods are susceptible to pilferage, the physical control over storage locations will be relied on to make up for the lack of adequate financial records of stock movements.

**6.07** Food stocks at the balance-sheet date will typically be valued at their latest invoice price. This treatment is likely to be acceptable because the quantity of food held at any one time will not be so great that any changes in price since the food was purchased will significantly affect the hotel's financial results.

**6.08** Food stocks will not normally be held long enough to be subject to deterioration, so that it will be unusual for those stocks to be reflected in the balance sheet at their realisable value.

*Beverages*

**6.09** Many hotels maintain substantial stocks of wines. These stocks are likely to appreciate over time, but even so they should be valued at the lower of cost (on a first-in, first-out basis) and net-realisable value. Control over wines and spirits is almost always strict, because these stocks constitute the largest component of hotel stocks by value and, like food, they are susceptible to pilferage. Stores records will be maintained from goods received notes and internal issue notes. Stocks should be counted monthly, and the book stock should be regularly reconciled to the physical stock using the bin cards.

**6.10** Bar stocks are normally controlled on either a daily or a weekly basis by charging issues to the bar at selling price, deducting the takings, and comparing the balance with a physical count valued at selling price.

**6.11** Beverage stocks at the balance-sheet date should be valued at cost; some wines may deteriorate, and the advice of the professional stocktaker (see 6.16 below) should be sought in this regard. Also wines may be removed from the wine lists from time to time, and when this happens a provision for the diminution in their value may be necessary.

*Linen, silverware, china and glass*

**6.12** The physical controls and the documentation dealing with the movement of reserve stocks of linen, silverware, china and glass will be similar to those for beverages. Issues should be made only infrequently from the store, but high-value items should be counted regularly. Where complete records are maintained the stocks should be counted annually, and should be valued at cost.

**6.13** Where a hotel is not currently using some of its stocks of linen, silverware, china and glass there are three possible accounting treatments for those stocks. They may either be treated as fixed assets, or be written-off on acquisition, or be treated as an operating asset (i.e. stock). Some entities capitalise the initial cost of equipping a hotel with its linen, silverware, glass and china, and then write-off replacement supplies as and when they are issued from the reserve stores. When these items are significant, an accounting policy note should explain the treatment adopted.

*Maintenance and general stores*

**6.14** Expenditure incurred on maintenance and repairs may be substantial, particularly in older hotels. Control over maintenance materials and other general stores (such as stationery and cleaning materials) is, however, frequently poor. Bin cards or a stores ledger are not normally used to record stock movements, but where they are, and the quantities on hand are checked to these records periodically, the records may form the basis for the year-end valuation. These stores are usually valued for balance-sheet purposes at their latest invoice price. This treatment is generally acceptable, because of the immateriality of the amounts involved.

*Summary*

**6.15** A physical stocktaking is normally made at the year-end date and stocks are stated in the financial statements at the lower of cost and net-realisable value. Cost is ascertained on a first-in, first-out basis. For the fast-moving supplies, however, cost may be based on the prices that were current immediately prior to the year-end date. For reserve stocks, the cost will be the purchase price, as determined from perpetual inventory records (where these records are maintained). On rare occasions only, it will be necessary to provide against the cost of perishable food or wine.

**Audit considerations**

*The use of professional stocktakers and valuers*

**6.16** Because of the wide variety of items held in stock, a considerable amount of clerical effort is required to list and price year-end stocks. Also, skill and experience are required in order to identify and value cellar wines, especially those that may have deteriorated. Therefore, many hotels use professional stocktakers and valuers for preparing the year-end stock figures.

**6.17** The use of professional stocktakers and valuers does not relieve the auditor of his responsibility for establishing the truth and fairness of the inventory valuation. However, it may well enable him to limit the extent of his work. A meeting with the stocktaker should be arranged, and his laid-down procedures should be reviewed and evaluated. The auditor should also attend the counts of categories of stock that he judges to be material, to establish that the laid-down procedures are implemented. The auditor should seek the advice of the professional stocktaker in assessing the adequacy of any stock provisions that may be necessary.

*Stock at outside locations*

**6.18** As mentioned above, larger hotels may have a substantial investment in wines held by producers, in spirits at the distillers, and in both wines and spirits held in bonded stores. Frozen goods may also be held in bulk storage either at the supplier's premises, or elsewhere. Records should be available of the initial cost of such supplies, and also of subsequent expenditure for storage, insurance and carriage. The auditor must, however, obtain independent confirmation from the custodian of both the ownership and the existence of the stocks, as well as the details of any lien or charge that the custodian exercises over the goods.

**Current cost accounting**

**6.19** The application of current cost accounting techniques to hotel stocks should cause few problems. It will normally be possible to apply conventional methods to most categories of stock to arrive at the cost of sales adjustment and the value to the business of the stock.

**6.20** The matters most likely to cause problems are:

(a) The treatment of wine stocks;

(b) The treatment of china, glass and silverware which are accounted for as stock.

**6.21** Wine will normally be stated in the current cost balance sheet at the replacement cost of a current year's wine of similar quality. However, where establishments have a policy of partially replacing with identical wine, replacement cost will include an element that reflects the rarity value of the wine. The cost of sales adjustment will normally be calculated by means of the averaging method. An internal price index may be devised which is based on the hotel's normal buying policy. It may also be necessary to write the stock down to net-realisable value because of possible deterioration.

**6.22** China, glass and silverware will normally be stated in the current cost balance sheet by reference to specific replacement cost or appropriate indices. Where establishments would replace old valuable items, for example antiques, with similar, again the value to the business will include an element that reflects the rarity value of the items. As with wines, the cost of sales adjustment will normally be calculated by means of the averaging method and an internal price index may be devised which is based on the hotel's normal replacement policy.

**6.23** Where stocks are held largely for the purpose of achieving a holding gain, it may not be appropriate to revalue stock in the current cost balance sheet and to calculate a cost of sales adjustment. In such cases the stock should be included in the current cost balance sheet on the historical cost basis and be included in the calculation of the monetary working capital adjustment.

# JEWELLERY
## S. Ingram

---

### Background to the business

**7.01** The jewellery trade in the United Kingdom comprises a wide range of businesses which have seen many developments over the past few years. The retail sector has seen increasing penetration by a small number of large multiple groups which are very marketing-conscious and have increased the fashion element of the business significantly. Additionally non-jewellery retailers, including discount chains, are endeavouring to break into the retail jewellery market by opening jewellery departments in their stores. The wholesale sector has declined in importance whilst the manufacturing sector has had to contend with the boom and slump conditions which have prevailed. Meanwhile there has been a marked increase in the level of import activity.

**7.02** In spite of these developments, the UK jewellery trade remains highly fragmented, comprising a large, though diminishing, number of independent business enterprises still run largely as small businesses.

**7.03** Throughout the 1970s the jewellery business showed a steady rate of growth apart from a hiccough in 1973/4 which was precipitated by a change in the rate of VAT. However, in the late 1970s and early 1980s this sector experienced significant volatility in the price levels of first of all diamonds, and then precious metals. The price of gold in particular has risen substantially during times of political and economic unrest and then declined as soon as each crisis is over. As there is no indication of an end to such unsettled periods, price levels will presumably continue to be volatile.

### Accounting considerations

**7.04** It goes without saying that the existence and the extent of accounting (and therefore auditing) problems will be dependent on the quality of the internal controls and accounting records of the business. It is also relevant to mention that most jewellers are conscious of the high value of their stocks and the need to ensure that stock is properly controlled. Thus even in a small business, although there may not appear to be a formal stock-recording system, there may be an informal system, maintained by a director, but on which the auditor is able to place some reliance.

**7.05** The accounting problems that are likely to be encountered arise for the reasons set out below.

**7.06** The business of a retail jeweller is a cash business. Even manufacturers and wholesalers may transact some of their business for cash. Thus transactions may not be properly recorded (or even recorded at all) and this can be expected to affect the reliability of other aspects of the accounting systems, e.g. VAT records, stock records. Furthermore, purchases of secondhand jewellery are often for cash. It is important in such transactions that, to protect his own commercial interests, the jeweller should maintain proper records of all transactions. When secondhand jewellery is being purchased from the public, there should be a proper system to ensure that a pre-numbered receipt is signed by the seller to state that the item being sold is his or her own property and that he/she is not registered for VAT purposes.

**7.07** The ready portability of jewellery combined with the ease with which it may be concealed means that the jeweller must ensure that he has proper day-to-day control over his stocks. Various systems exist to achieve this objective, including:

(a) detailed stock records;

(b) carrying out weekly checks on hash totals of jewellery by type, e.g. wedding rings, or single stone diamond rings;

(c) opening stock, adjusted for goods received, goods sold and transfers should equal physical stock;

(d) imprest control via standard display pads (the shop carries a predetermined stock, and a gap on a pad must mean that an item has been sold).

Nevertheless the danger of theft will always be present and the jeweller must guard against it.

**7.08** Scrap will arise in all jewellery manufacturing companies and also those which carry out any repair activity which involves the use of precious metals. Accordingly, a proper procedure should be set up to ensure that all scrap is accounted for, and that opportunities for pilferage are eliminated.

**7.09** Manufacturing companies normally have security screening for all employees entering and leaving the production area. It is also normal to provide specific overalls for employees, and when these overalls are to be thrown out they are sold to the smelters, as particles of gold inevitably accumulate. In fact, all aspects of jewellery workshop activity result in the accumulation of scrap which is saleable. Thus workshops are cleaned at frequent intervals and all the dust collected in the dust extraction system as well as all the dust and dirt collected in the vacuum cleaner etc. should be carefully collected and sold to a smelting company. Companies should therefore control all scrap in an appropriate manner and ensure that sales to the smelting company are properly accounted for.

**7.10** The main problem of valuation arises if it is not possible to relate stock to its purchase cost. This is particularly relevant with non-branded items, for example gems, gem set jewellery etc., where it is not possible to turn to a price list or catalogue to check a price.

It would appear that the only way to overcome this problem is to set up a reliable stock-recording system (see paragraphs 7.12–7.19 below).

**7.11** Although many jewellery companies are small in terms of numbers of employees and so can perhaps be expected to display only limited internal control procedures, there is a countervailing force. This is the complexity of many jewellery businesses, which, together with the large capital requirements, will greatly motivate the directors to ensure that all aspects of the business are tightly controlled.

**Stock control**

**7.12** In any jewellery business, be it a manufacturer, importer, retailer or precious stone dealer, a substantial proportion of capital will be tied up in stock. Accordingly, the key to the profitability of the business will of necessity hinge on proper stock utilisation, i.e. reliable information on the amounts tied up in different categories of stock as well as details of stock movements. It is therefore essential for the jeweller to operate a proper stock-control system, to provide both management information and management control.

**7.13** Most jewellery businesses probably operate some form of stock-control system, even though it may be rudimentary, which could be formalised. In the case of a business where the stock is basically high value and the volume of sales is low, this should cause little administrative difficulty. If the volume of turnover is high, a proper stock-control system may well be more difficult to maintain but will be just as essential.

**7.14** The stock-recording system should enable ready reference between individual items and the stock records. Accordingly it will be necessary for each item of stock to carry some form of identification tag or marking.

The use of such tags or markings should be carefully controlled. Shown below is an example of an index card which may be used in a simple stock system in a wholesale or retail company. It could also be used for recording finished goods in a manufacturing business. This system could be readily adapted to computer application.

<table>
<tr><td colspan="6" rowspan="2">Supplier: Name<br>Address<br><br>Tel. No.</td><td colspan="2">Stock No.</td></tr>
<tr><td colspan="2">Description</td></tr>
<tr><td colspan="8">Special instructions</td></tr>
<tr><td rowspan="2">Date</td><td rowspan="2">Purchase invoice no.</td><td colspan="3">Quantity</td><td rowspan="2">Cost excl. VAT</td><td rowspan="2">Retail excl. VAT</td><td rowspan="2">Retail incl. VAT</td></tr>
<tr><td>In</td><td>Out</td><td>Bal</td></tr>
<tr><td></td><td></td><td></td><td></td><td></td><td></td><td></td><td></td></tr>
</table>

In a business which has large premises or more than one location it would normally be necessary also to show the location of the stock. In a large business which carries large stocks of similar items, significant benefits could be derived from computerising stock records.

**7.15** The stock number could be coded in such a way that all stock cards are in supplier order, for example purchases from John Black could be coded JB1, JB2 etc. This would provide considerable advantages when re-ordering takes place, and also in recording the receipt of goods. This card-index system could be easily adapted to the needs of a manufacturing company, although precious metals should be controlled on a weight basis. Instead of the stock (prior to manufacture) carrying a stock-number tag, it would be necessary for regular test weighings to take place to ensure that usage is being properly controlled.

**7.16** The reliability of any stock-control system is dependent upon the quality of information relating to purchases, sales and transfers, for example from raw materials to work-in-progress. Accordingly it will be necessary to ensure that not only all purchases are entered on the relevant cards but also that all sales are properly recorded at the time of sale, and subsequently entered on the stock records. The purchase invoice number should be recorded on the stock-control card to facilitate cross-reference.

**7.17** Normally, it would not be cost effective for such a stock system to include low-value items such as watch straps, watch components, jewellers' sundries, for example ring clips and safety chains, unless these happened to form a large proportion of the value of stock held by the business.

**7.18** When items are held on a sale or return basis, they should be clearly and separately recorded. This could be done quite easily by giving such stock items a prefix or suffix letter code, for example items held on sale or return from John Brown could be coded JBA, the 'A' indicating that the item is on sale or return.

**7.19** Conversely stock which is held by customers (e.g. retail jewellers) but which remains the property of the manufacturer should also be properly controlled. This should involve periodic returns from the customer:

(a) at least monthly, giving details of goods sold;

(b) quarterly, confirming stocks unsold.

**Measurement of profit**

**7.20** Once a stock-control system has been set up, it is an easy step to produce management accounts. For example, the stock-control system outlined above readily lends itself to the production of periodic management accounts (weekly or monthly) or at least a calculation of the gross profit of a business. This can be done merely by including a gross profit column in the sales day book.

**7.21** Thus by listing the stock number sold, the sales figures and the gross profit on each transaction, (which can easily be arrived at by deducting cost price from sales price) a considerable amount of management information is derived.

| | | Sales Day Book | | |
|---|---|---|---|---|
| *Date* | *Stock No.* | *Sales price incl VAT* | *VAT* | *Gross profit* |
| 1st June | JB 7 | 46.00 | 6.00 | 15.00 |
| 1st June | PR 114 | 125.00 | 16.30 | 47.00 |
| 1st June | BS 83 | 9.00 | 1.17 | 3.85 |
| | | etc. | | |

The jeweller is then able to refer to his sales day book not only to see which items are selling, but also to identify where he is earning his profit.

## Auditing problems

**7.22** The audit of stocks held by jewellers poses one of the more difficult problems presented to auditors. Few items have the combination of portability and immensely concentrated value of jewellery. There are obviously traps and snares for the unwary. How does the auditor know that the diamond he has been shown is not merely a piece of glass? Is the alleged 'gold' bracelet, just a cheap alloy? The auditor obviously cannot expect to possess the expert knowledge to be able to answer problems such as these, but by combining the information provided by the client's systems and general background knowledge of the jewellery business, most difficulties can normally be overcome.

**7.23** The audit approach will obviously vary significantly especially in cases where the stock falls into one of the following categories:

(a) readily-identifiable branded items, e.g. watches, clocks, cutlery, glassware;

(b) one-off hand made pieces of precious jewellery;

(c) high fashion goods.

However, in all cases it is of over-riding importance that the stock is subject to a proper stock-recording system.

**7.24** Reference has already been made to systems of internal control. The auditor should apply the same sort of techniques to the audit of jewellery companies as he does to all other audits. Thus if he wishes to rely on internal controls then he must first review and assess the procedures relating to stocks. Where the auditor decides that there are internal controls on which he may rely, he should proceed with his audit on that basis. In cases where he feels unable to rely on internal controls, then an increased level of substantive testing will be required.

**7.25** In any event, certain basic tests will require to be carried out:

(a) attendance at stocktaking; in a company with more than one branch it may well be that a full physical stocktake is not carried out at the balance-sheet date and reliance is therefore based on the stock records. In this situation it is essential to prove the accuracy of stock records by compliance tests and also to carry out spot checks at the balance sheet date;

(b) review the client's procedures for, and control over, stocktaking;

(c) establish the reliability of procedures over items which should be excluded from stock, for example:

 (i) stock held on sale or return;

 (ii) items held for customers for repair and safekeeping;

 (iii) the procedures applied to stock items where a deposit has been paid and a balance is outstanding;

(d) when stock is held by third parties, for example on sale or return, the auditor should carry out a review of sales, items returned, and items which are held by third parties at the year-end and have been in the third parties' possession for a significant period of time. Additionally, as part of the audit planning, consideration should be given to the need to carry out a visit to any third party who holds a material amount of a client's stock or the need to obtain certificates of confirmation direct from them.

**Genuineness**

**7.26** Thus it should be possible to establish that stock exists and to agree the physical stock to the stock records. But what about its genuineness? For example, is something which is described as 'gold' actually gold?

The genuineness of a stock item (especially in the case of rings, ear-rings, brooches etc. where the item is set with gemstones) cannot normally be established by the inexpert auditor. A 'diamond ring' being carried in stock at its cost price of £5,000 may in fact be a ring with a simulated diamond which costs only £50. This problem is exacerbated by the fact that individual high-value items can be easily concealed and are readily transported.

**7.27** Test checks should be carried out by the auditor to see that items which should be hallmarked have been. This is a complex area, but basically all gold, silver and platinum of current manufacture (including gem-set jewellery) should be hallmarked.

**7.28** The law is set out in the Hallmarking Act 1973 as amended by the Hallmarking (Exempted Articles) (Amendment) Order 1975 (Statutory Instrument 1975 No. 1883). A hallmark is made up of four constituent parts:

(a) the sponsor's mark. Each sponsor has his own mark which is approved by and registered with the British Hallmarking Council;

(b) the standard mark. This indicates whether the item is silver, platinum or gold and the quality of the precious metal, for example '375' represents nine carat gold. (Nine carat is nine parts in 24 which equals .375.) It is possible, by looking at the standard mark, to establish whether the article is British or imported, for example if a gold article is of British manufacture, a crown appears before the standard of the gold;

(c) the assay office mark, for example the Yorkshire rose for the Sheffield assay office;

(d) the date letter: A = 1975
B = 1976
C = 1977 etc.

**7.29** It may be possible to use expertise which exists within the client's business, and so for example, if the client has a few shops, area managers and branch managers could be swapped around between branches to supervise the stocktaking of another branch. In larger organisations, the auditor may be able to obtain assistance from the client's specialist staff when seeking reassurance on the genuineness of items.

**7.30** Obviously, looking at the proposed selling prices of articles and comparing these with cost will provide some evidence of the genuineness of items, as will carrying out test checks on the prices at which transactions have taken place after the balance-sheet date compared with the proposed selling price.

**Valuation**

**7.31** In a business which has a reliable stock-recording system, most of the problems of valuation are automatically overcome, provided that prices are not fluctuating and that margins are high. It has been seen above how it is readily possible to agree physical stock with book stock. It then becomes a simple task to evaluate the stock, so long as the cost price has been recorded in the stock records. In cases of doubt or query, and also as a normal part of the auditor's tests, it is possible to trace back to original invoices.

**7.32** The remaining problems will be:

(a) slow-moving stocks, and net-realisable value;

(b) scrap stocks;

(c) loose stones.

**Slow-moving stocks and net-realisable value**

**7.33** One feature of the jewellery trade is that stocks move slowly. However, historically, unless the stock was high fashion, the general rise in prices of gold, diamonds etc. and the high margins usually encountered in the trade has meant that slow-moving stocks do not normally present a large problem for the auditor. Nevertheless it is not a matter which should be ignored, particularly when considering clocks, watches and other branded items, and also taking into account price fluctuations in gold, precious stones and silver.

**Scrap stocks**

**7.34** The auditor will need to ensure that all scrap stocks are properly included in the stocktake. This will normally involve weighing these stocks in their separate categories, for example silver, 9 carat gold, 18 carat gold. It should then prove relatively easy to arrive at a cost price for valuing this scrap stock by reference to the approximate buying price of gold/scrap gold. A margin for error is usually acceptable on this aspect of stock valuation as the sums involved are not normally material to the total stock valuation.

**Loose stones**

**7.35** In arriving at the valuation attributed to loose stones, the auditor is highly dependent on the reliance he is able to place on the company's systems. It is therefore essential to ensure that the company operates adequate systems and the auditor should establish their reliability by appropriate tests.

**General**

**7.36** It has been suggested that, in cases of difficulty, independent professional stock valuers could be used to perform the stocktake. However, it has not proved possible to identify a firm of valuers who are able to provide stock valuation which will accord with SSAP 9, i.e. at the lower of cost and net-realisable value.

**7.37** As the graph opposite indicates, there have been severe gold price fluctuations during the period late 1979 to mid 1981 and such market conditions are likely to give rise to problems which have not been experienced during recent history.

**7.38** Furthermore, what has been happening to gold has also been happening to diamonds (to a lesser extent), and with the advent of increasing price competition and fashion influences, especially in watches, the

*Source: Financial Times*

auditor will need to be more alert to the likelihood that net-realisable value may be less than cost and so provisions may need to be made in valuing stock.

**7.39** Thus the volatility of the price of gold and sterling together with the increasing element of fashion and price competition which is entering into the jewellery business will require the auditor to adapt his tests to conditions which have not prevailed in the jewellery sector in the recent past. He will be concerned with slow-moving and obsolete stocks, problems relating to net-realisable value (especially on low-margin goods) and in the case of individual items of precious jewellery he may even be concerned with scrap values.

**Materiality**

**7.40** The auditor may also have problems in setting his materiality levels; in an extreme case, one item might account for 10 per cent, 20 per cent or possibly even 30 per cent of stock by value, and its omission from stock or its incorrect inclusion in stock would obviously have a significant impact on the stated results for the period under review. However, it would be unusual for so much of the value of a jeweller's stock to be tied up in one item.

**7.41** Paragraphs 14–21 explained how a simple management accounts system could be established. Such a system should enable the auditor to carry out an effective analytical review and so would assist significantly in ensuring that there are no major omissions from stock. Similarly, it should help provide reassurance that no items are included in stock which should not have been included, for example sale-or-return items. Nevertheless the incidence of very variable margins in the trade, arising from such factors as inflation in the selling price of stocks, volume discounts, and the expertise of the buyer, should be borne in mind by the auditor when carrying out his review.

**Conclusion**

**7.42** What is clear is that a combination of pressures should ensure that the jeweller maintains sound records. The pressures include the requirement to keep proper records for VAT purposes, the Companies Act 1976 and even more importantly the recognition that the considerable sums tied up in a jeweller's stock require good housekeeping.

**7.43** What is even more clear is that provided the jewellery company has sound systems then with a reasonable knowledge of the jewellery business (but without the need for specialist knowledge) the auditor should be able to overcome most problems which arise in the audit of jewellery companies.

# TANNING AND FINISHING INDUSTRY

D. I. Stewart and D. R. Philip

### Background to the business

**8.01** This chapter deals with the principles and problems of the valuation of leather products during processing from the raw-skin stage to the finished skin which is ready for making up into products such as shoes, clothing and gloving. There are several firms in the UK involved in this intermediate state of production. Usually particular firms will concentrate on different types of raw material which can be made up into finished leather, for example bovines, which may be used where thicker leather is required, such as for shoes. Sheep and goat skins are used where a more supple, finer leather is required, as in gloving and for certain clothing. Many other types of hide/skin (such as crocodile/elephant) are lumped together under the name of 'exotics' and tend to be used largely for clothing. The production of different types of skin is often concentrated in separate firms or plants because the exact processes involved differ with the types of skin used.

### Production processes

**8.02** To illustrate the types of processes involved it may be helpful to examine a firm that deals in the tanning and finishing of sheep and goat skins.

**8.03** As preparation before tanning, the skins are dehaired, any remaining flesh is removed and if necessary the skins are split. Splitting occurs if the skin is too thick in relation to the final product. The outside of the skins (sometimes known as grains or skivers) are used for shoes, gloving and for decorative leather work such as table tops. The inside of the skin is used as a suede or chamois effect for cheaper clothing or shoes. The skins are then tanned which involves pickling and softening ready for finishing. When the skins have been tanned they are dried, and they have then reached a stage at which the quality can be reasonably assessed. The skins are sorted by reference to their thickness and quality, and stored in readiness for issue to later stages of production based on the requirement of customer orders.

**8.04** These later stages of production involve dyeing the skins, applying a finish (for example matt, sheen or peccary), then further softening, plus trimming and reducing the skins to an even thickness. The skins are then sorted based on colour and quality in order to check whether the batch of processed skins still meets the quality required for an order.

**8.05** Control over the number of skins is difficult as certain types of skins are subject to splitting and others may be spoilt in the production process. To allow for this, conditions in the leather trade generally allow a 10 per cent variation in both quantity and quality of skins delivered against orders.

**8.06** Processes in the production of finished bovine skins are similar to those outlined above, but the skins are split to the width that is required before processing. The 'insides' of skins are referred to as 'splits' and are not of great value.

**8.07** The process cycle is fairly lengthy, and from input of raw skins into tanning to the production of finished skins a time span of between five and eight weeks is quite common.

**Other business considerations**

**8.08** The UK tanning and leather industry is heavily reliant on imports of raw skins, thus costs are subject to foreign currency fluctuations and to the problem of political instability in developing countries – traditional suppliers of hides and skins. The advance of leather producing industries in the developing countries has led to a reduction in available supplies of raw skins and increased (often subsidised) competition in finished skins.

**8.09** These factors, together with the vagaries of supply and demand have resulted in highly volatile price movements. In early 1979 prices of hides rocketed as Russian and Far Eastern buyers increased their purchases at a time when the supply of raw hides from South America was being cut back. By mid 1979, however, largely as a result of above average cattle slaughters in the EEC, together with a drop in purchasing by Russia and the Far Eastern countries, hide prices fell. The extent of this volatility was seen in 1980 with hide prices falling from 70p to 30p a kilo, before recovering in 1981 to around 50p a kilo.

**8.10** Hide prices are often geared more to market conditions than to foreign currency fluctuations, but these play an important part in influencing the level of sales and margins obtainable. Exports account for around 40 per cent of turnover of the major British manufacturers. When sterling in 1980 was above $2, it became more difficult to export to the lucrative United States and Canadian markets. It also resulted in greater competition within the UK with cheaper imports of leather and leather goods from developing countries. The fall in sterling against the dollar and other currencies during 1981 increased competitiveness both abroad and in the UK market.

## Accounting and auditing problems

*Physical Existence*

**8.11** The valuation of stock begins with the establishment of the physical nature and ownership of stock held. The physical nature of the stocks from raw skins, through partly processed leather to finished goods, and the large number of processes involved makes accurate physical stocktaking difficult. This difficulty is amplified by the large volumes of stock held (in relation to other assets) resulting from two main factors:

(a) the relatively long process cycle which results in a large element of work-in-progress;

(b) fluctuating raw material prices which can lead to large quantities being purchased to safeguard supplies and as a hedge against adverse price movements.

In these circumstances a good system of stock control is essential, helping not only to establish total quantities but also to identify through which of the many processes the skin has passed.

**8.12** At the year-end careful consideration will be needed to determine the cut-off point between production processes, given the large quantities and number of processes involved. Raw skins-in-transit are often a particular problem in cut-off at the year-end as difficulties may arise in ascertaining the exact date on which title passed and, if the firm regularly receives large shipments from abroad, this aspect may be material.

*Cost of production*

**8.13** The next stage in valuation involves establishing the cost of production of finished goods and particularly work-in-progress. Many firms produce largely to order, and this coupled with a long processing cycle means that work-in-progress usually forms a significant part of stock at the year-end.

**8.14** Costs incurred must therefore be ascertained for both finished stock and also for each stage of production. To assist in this many companies have developed a process-based standard costing system – and the existence of such can significantly aid the year-end valuation of stock. However, the relatively long process cycle and the large number of processes, many of them depending on the particular quality of the leather required, may have made it necessary to aggregate certain operations. As in all cases where a standard costing system is used in the valuation, the auditor will need to review the results and accuracy of the information produced by the system and in particular consider:

(a) the method of costing; (b) the costs absorbed; (c) the level of activity over which the costs are absorbed; and (d) the variances arising from the system.

In this the level of activity is of particular importance given the cyclical nature of the industry.

**8.15** The large number of processes is not the only complication in the apportionment of process (or total) costs. Quality control is a particular problem in the leather industry. When the hide is purchased there is little indication of the eventual quality which will be achieved and the hide can initially only be graded in very broad terms. Once the leather has reached a certain stage of production it can be graded, but then a decision must be made as to how both hide and process costs are to be apportioned over a large number of different grades of leather. If costs are apportioned evenly but demand for different grades of leather is uneven, then this could lead to greater complications in the comparison of cost to net-realisable value – especially if lower grades of leather are a disproportionate part of stock held at the year-end.

**8.16** The decision on cost apportionment could have a significant effect on profits, and this is aggravated when stock levels are changing in total or by component. For example, if the higher grades are held in stock at the year-end and lower grades are sold during the year – at lower selling prices – then the relationship of cost to selling price will have been relatively high and profits will consequently be lower than had the reverse been the case. This effect would be aggravated by a change in demand, for example, if in the previous year the lower grades had not been selling and had made up the greater part of the stock.

**8.17** Costs could, of course, be apportioned in relation to selling price, but this is not without its problems. A change in demand leading to a change in selling price would lead to a change in cost structure. This method of cost apportionment would also conceal information about the relative profitability of different lines/grades from management. For this reason, some firms in the industry prefer to value stock based on selling price rather than attributable cost.

*Valuation based on selling price*

**8.18** Certain firms in the industry diverge from the usual method of building up the cost of stocks and work-in-progress and instead determine their value by reference to selling prices, less appropriate profit margins, selling costs and other costs to be incurred. The reason is that once the skin reaches a particular stage in the production cycle the original raw material tends to lose its identity and hence its 'cost'. At this stage it is the nature of the finished leather which is most important, and the value of the skin is no longer related to the costs incurred but rather is dependent on the quality that the skin will achieve when finished. One advantage of this method of valuation is that stock will automatically reflect net-realisable value. It is particularly relevant where there is a large divergence in the quality of skins received from production, and as a result a large divergence in the potential sale proceeds.

**8.19** The audit problem arising from this method of valuation is to consider whether it accords with SSAP 9. The explanatory note to SSAP 9 gives an example of the use of a 'selling-price-minus' basis in the case of retail stores where this may be the only practical method of arriving at a figure which approximates to cost. The auditor will need to consider, on the facts of each case, whether this is really the only practical method available, or whether a build up of cost is possible. It may be that a build up of cost *would* be possible but the more practical method is to use the 'selling-price-minus' basis. In this case the auditor may be able to build up his own assessment of cost in aggregate to compare to the valuation on the 'selling-price-minus' basis, to obtain a view on the reasonableness of the stock valuation as a whole.

**8.20** The problems involved with a valuation based on cost, as outlined in paragraphs 8.13 to 8.17 above, may mean, that a valuation based on selling price could give a fairer view of the value of stock held at the year-end.

*Consideration of net-realisable value*

**8.21** Stock valued on the 'selling-price-minus' basis will automatically reflect net-realisable value where selling price is based on finished quality. When cost is used as a basis for valuing stock then net-realisable value will need to be separately considered. The quality achieved from production will need to be used to evaluate net-realisable value for comparison with the cost of stock held at the year-end.

**8.22** The quality achieved from production used in this comparison should ideally be that which applies to the stock and work-in-progress at the year-end. This may not always be possible, however, as, at the time net-realisable value is being considered, items in year-end work-in-progress may not have been completed. For this reason, previous records of production quality achieved may have to be used to assess the quality of skins still in production (this applies to stock valued on both 'cost' and 'selling-price' bases). There should be no problem in determining the quality of finished stock as this should already have been graded.

**8.23** Regardless of the method of valuation used, a further adjustment to reflect net-realisable value may be required for grades of leather produced which are not in great demand, unless the company's pricing policy already reflects this position. This is a particular problem in the leather industry for two reasons:

(a) The company may have little control over the actual grades of leather produced from skins put into production. This is compensated for, to some extent, by the usual conditions of trade allowing a 10 per cent variation in quality and quantity either side of the customer's order, but in spite of this there may be an increasing volume of goods held, not linked specifically to orders.

(b) Not all grades of leather are in the same demand. To take an example from the gloving leather industry, higher grades may be used for quality gloving, lower grades may be used for an imitation peccary finish which can conceal faults in the leather, but medium-quality leather may suffer from a lack of demand. This could be overcome by a suitable pricing policy, but if the company were to mark down the price of the medium-quality grades then it could well suffer an overall fall in its gross profit margin. Thus it may be difficult to maintain a pricing policy that avoids the stockpiling of certain grades and the auditor will need to review carefully the stock position, prices and order levels for each grade of leather.

(c) The movement of hide (skin) prices will also need to be reviewed in considering the net-realisable value, and this is particularly the case in the leather industry because of the extreme volatility of hide prices. If the price of hide falls, this is not automatically a reason to write-down stock values, providing the company can still continue to produce at a profit using the hides at the old price. The responsiveness of the company's selling price to its raw materials will need to be considered and also the extent to which its market share enables the company to resist a fall in selling prices. An adjustment to reduce cost to net-realisable value may be required following a fall in hide prices where the company is buying hides for resale.

**Conclusion**

**8.24** The basic principles of stock valuation which apply generally are still applicable to stock valuation in the leather industry. Certain aspects, however, become even more important where the processes and business environment are perhaps unfamiliar.

**8.25** It follows that an understanding is needed of the business environment in an industry which may be sensitive to political and social influences. For example, the industry may be very susceptible to political decisions by developing nations as to the export of raw hides. Internal political decisions may also severely affect particular companies in the industry, as witnessed by the legal action that was taken by a group of independent tanners to prevent subsidies being given to a particular tanner. Social influences may also affect the way in which firms are able to produce; an illustration of which is the pressure brought on firms in the leather industry to find an effective substitute for whale oil used in the softening of leather. Management decisions on future methods of production may be influenced by such political and social factors.

**8.26** Further, an understanding of the production processes is necessary to understand the make-up of stock and work-in-progress. In undertaking a review of the valuation it is essential to be aware of the inherent problems of stock valuation in this industry:

(a) the large number of processes involved (which will vary depending on quality and required finish), with the consequent difficulties of apportioning process costs;

(b) the loss of identity of the original raw material, and hence its 'cost' at a particular state in the production cycle, following which stage the nature of the finished leather becomes most important.

(c) the problems of controlling quality, and the effect of varying qualities held and the method of apportioning costs on the valuation;

(d) the problems of fluctuating raw material prices.

# PUBLISHING

M. K. Down

## Background to the business

**9.01** The variety of forms which publishing can take is considerable. There is a common business basis which may be described as the preparation, marketing and sale to the public of the writing of an individual, whether an author, journalist, or indeed an advertiser. In most of its forms, publishing involves marketing to a substantial degree, in some cases to the extent of endeavouring to match or create a consumer demand to meet the supply. Within the confines of one chapter, it will be necessary to limit the description of various forms of publishing businesses. In terms of stock valuation, three examples have been chosen which are intended as a guide, namely:

(a) General publications made by selection of authors' works, editing, printing and marketing the titles to the public through wholesale and retail outlets;

(b) Technical publications as handbooks;

(c) Magazines, technical journals and newspapers.

**9.02** The accounting and auditing problems attached to these different examples are examined under their particular headings in the rest of this chapter.

## General publications

**9.03** Whilst newspapers, magazines and some journals have a regular publishing cycle to readers who do not vary to any large degree in number, or in nature between one publication and the next, general publishing has no such pattern. Each new title involves a separate assessment of its likely popularity. To obtain a reasonable costing and eventual selling price, the order to the printer will have to be for a sufficiently large number of copies to spread the fixed composing and setting-up costs.

**9.04** In general terms, the success of a publishing house may be related to its ability to attract successful authors by providing the service they need, and by having the ability to market successfully the titles they produce. In financial terms however, the profit or loss of a publishing house can depend upon the successful judgement of the number of copies of each title which can be sold. Too few copies means lost sales and expensive re-prints. More importantly, too many copies means wasted copies, fit only for pulp or remaindering. The major problem area in terms of stock valuation is the estimation of the net-realisable value and the consideration of whether this exceeds cost.

**9.05** The assessment of the saleability of book stocks is all important to the publisher, and is of concern to auditor and tax inspector alike. Methods of assessment of future sales and surplus stocks vary from a subjective judgement of the market for each title in turn, to the use of complex formulae. No answer will be correct and values will vary according to the optimism or otherwise of the valuer.

**9.06** Accountants of publishing houses and their auditors must devote a substantial amount of their time and attention to this vexed question of net-realisable value of unsold stocks and are obliged to rely to a degree on the assessment by the publisher of the whim of the eventual purchaser in the bookshop, or station bookstall, at some time in the future.

**9.07** Examination of a typical sequence of events within a general publishing house and the accumulation of stock value will demonstrate why estimation of net-realisable value is the major problem.

**9.08** On the decision to publish an author's work, an agreement is entered into with the author which, *inter alia*, will specify details of royalties and advance payment in expectation of royalties, design, printing and size of the first edition and whether publication will be in hardback, paperback or both. At this stage a costing and market sales analysis is made, leading to the critical decision as to the number of copies for the first edition and the publication date.

**9.09** On the placing of a contract with the printer (or printing division), paper is purchased and these direct costs are analysed to the new title. They will include costs of dust covers, packaging etc., but will usually exclude editorial and design costs which will be incorporated with an overhead oncost. Normally, royalty advances to authors will be treated as sales expenses as will other marketing costs. It will be seen that with proper analysis and an acceptable apportionment of editorial, design and other overheads, the problems of the accountant and the auditor are not difficult to this stage.

**9.10** While editing, printing and binding are proceeding, marketing arrangements are also being made, including advertising. Some weeks prior to the proposed publication date, the major sales effort is made to wholesalers and retailers. In the case of hardbacks particularly, the target is to sell prior to the publication date between 70 and 90 per cent of the number of copies printed. On the publication day, the second wave of advertising will be made, this time to the public, to coincide with the display of the title on the bookshelves of booksellers.

**9.11** It will be appreciated that the highest stock value for a title will be reached prior to the major sales effort to wholesalers and retailers. Accumulated costs will be accounted for but no test of the market can be made in terms of sales. Fortunately for accountants and auditors alike, the sales effort to wholesalers and retailers will be imminent and it will be possible for the auditor at least to examine, after the accounting date, the success or otherwise of pre-publication sales. Should pre-publication sales have fallen below expectation, consideration will have to be given to the saleability or realisable value of pre-publication stocks.

**9.12** On the assumption that the assessment by the publisher months earlier was accurate, immediately after publication date it is likely that only 10 to 30 per cent of the original printing order will remain in stock to meet orders and re-orders from booksellers. This stock may increase where the initial sales have been made with an agreement to re-purchase booksellers' unwanted stock as is customary.

**9.13** The realisable value of these residual stocks causes the greatest difficulty as has been indicated earlier. The publisher may argue, with good reason, that where a 90 per cent sale of a total print order is achieved and returns by customers' match orders in the first month or two after publication, and where there is no continuing re-order demand, the sales value of the remaining stock of the title is virtually nil.

**9.14** He may argue further that the disposal for pulp of a percentage of the print order will have been taken into account on setting the selling price and profit margin, and it may be far better to switch his sales effort to forthcoming publications. The stock of the title can remain in the warehouse and on the publication list for a certain period, depending on the nature of the book, but then it will be removed.

**9.15** The larger publishing house, in line with the above argument, may select a period of time (frequently between one and two years for hardback publications) and write-down stock values to nil over such a period; the argument being that out of, say, four dozen books remaining in stock 12 months after publication date, only two dozen will be sold. Others will review the stock lists with regard to the period elapsed since publication date, and sales made during that time, and take a subjective view as to the number of books of each title which will remain unsold on the decision to pulp.

**9.16** It is possible to adopt a reasonably systematic approach to such a review. The initial factors are factual, in terms of time and the pattern of monthly sales from which a future sales pattern may be projected and formulae may be produced. The process may be computerised. The subjective reviews by editorial and general management can be based on the results of the projections so calculated. The end result may be compared with actual sales up to the removal of the title from publication lists, and future projections modified from experience.

**9.17** It will be seen from the preceding paragraphs that, in a general publishing house, stocks remaining after publication date are likely to be but a small proportion of total stocks and an even smaller proportion of total sales. Nevertheless, their value can be considerable in relation to profit. While the publisher may find it practical and adequate to rely upon a set formula or method for the production of management accounts, the production and audit of year-end accounts may require closer scrutiny.

**Audit**

**9.18** From the audit viewpoint, the situation may be summarised as follows.

*Valuation*

**9.19**

(a) The compilation of costs for each title will form part of the accounting system and may be verified by normal audit techniques.

(b) Titles in process of printing have an accumulating value in terms of cost. This is frequently ignored, except where invoices have been received from printers and this has been included in stock value and purchases. Where an exceptionally large print order is in progress, confirmation of cost to date could be obtained, and incorporated in the accounts.

(c) Detailed consideration and examination of overhead additions to costs of stocks will be necessary as with other businesses, with the understanding that much of the expense connected with each publication relates to its marketing and sale and will therefore be excluded.

*Quantities*

**9.20**

(a) Stock quantities should be subject to normal audit procedures without difficulty; most publishers keep continuous stock records which will assist the verification.

(b) Bulk paper stocks not allocated to titles may be verified, frequently by certificate from paper mills or stockists, also from printers.

*Realisable values*

**9.21**

(a) The methods of valuation of remaining stocks will require detailed examination and consideration.

(b) Confirmation of the principles adopted should be obtained at board level; the same is true of any changes in principles and methods of valuation adopted.

(c) The principles and methods should be understood and tests made in detail to establish their application.

(d) Major items in stock and major write-downs in value should be subject to detailed scrutiny, discussion with publishers as to the sales progress, and examination of sales records after the accounting date.

(e) Similar tests should be made in respect of the titles selected at the end of the previous accounting period, to establish, over a minimum of 12 months, that the system of write-off had been reasonable. Where this was not the case, an adjustment may be necessary and, in any case, the methods used by the management should then be subject to further examination and enquiry.

(f) The method of assessment of returns to stock after the balance-sheet date in respect of sales prior to that date must be examined and tested, primarily to establish the value of the reduction in sales and profit in the accounting year but also to verify the additionals to stock value.

(g) Trading arrangements and terms with major customers should be examined in respect of the possibility of returns of unsold copies. The publisher will vary the treatment of stocks of returned unsold copies, depending on the likelihood of re-sale. Such stocks should in any event suffer the same audit scrutiny as remaining stocks for insaleability.

(h) Stock lists should be checked with the current publication list to ensure adequate write-off in respect of stocks of titles no longer listed. A similar check may be made with the publisher's planned future removals from the publication lists.

**9.22** The treatment of paperback stocks by a publisher will follow the pattern already described but will vary in certain aspects. A greater proportion of copies will be accepted on a sale-or-return basis. In certain cases, travelling representatives will re-stock the agreed space allotted to the publisher by the bookseller. Such re-stocking may be made from copies withdrawn from other booksellers in addition to supplying new titles.

**9.23** The attitude of publishers to returned paperback stocks varies. Some will pulp all such returns, as they consider that the cost of sorting, cleaning and re-racking or packing paperbacks to be greater than their value. Such a method has the advantage of enabling the publisher to consider all 'car stocks' of paperbacks of their representatives to be of no value, except possibly stocks of new titles.

**9.24** It is accepted that the sales life of the general paperback is approximately half that of a hardback title and stocks remaining after publication date are frequently reduced to nil over a 12-month period, prior to withdrawal from the publishing lists.

**9.25** One apparent anomaly can arise in reducing the value of stocks by one of the various methods described for writing-off apparently unsaleable stocks. Where a title continues to sell well or its initial sales exceed expectations, a re-print will be ordered. It is usual to restore written-down stocks to full value in such circumstances. However, the variances caused by such a procedure are comparatively small in most cases as stocks of such titles are usually low. The auditor should be aware of this possibility.

**9.26** A further anomaly arises when a hardback title is published at a later date as a paperback. Customer response will vary in such circumstances but the marketing effort accompanying the publication of the paperback frequently can cause an increase rather than a reduction in sales of the hardback, as might appear to be the more logical course of events. This may affect the valuation of the hardback stock.

**Taxation**

**9.27** The attitude of the Inland Revenue to the publisher's estimate of the number of copies of any title which will prove to be unsaleable, and the corresponding reduction in stock value, is not always the same as that of the publisher or the auditor. Reducing the value of stocks which continue to be sold does not conform to normal accounting or tax practice in other industries and there is a natural resistance to such a procedure.

**9.28** It is necessary to draw the attention of an Inspector of Taxes to the fact that stocks of a title remaining after publication date are only the remainder unsold following the main marketing effort, and are but a small proportion of the original total stock originally available for sale. His attention should also be drawn to the fact that the life cycle of a title is already several months old by the time the publication date is reached, and the publisher is not writing-off 'new stock'.

**Technical publications as handbooks**

**9.29** While many of the characteristics of publishing technical handbooks are similar to those for general publishing, certain different features may be identified.

**9.30** A technical publication often will comprise an edited work of several authors or contributors, who are likely to be paid fees which usually become part of the accumulating cost of a publication, as opposed to royalties to authors in respect of copies sold.

**9.31** The market for a technical publication will be restricted to a large degree to those with an interest in the subject matter and the forecast sales may be quantified with more accuracy in the case of handbooks and with considerable accuracy in the case of journals for which subscriptions are received or which are mailed free, the income arising from advertisements alone. Advertising revenue will also arise in many technical handbooks.

**9.32** Technical handbooks will often have a life planned by their publisher and will be succeeded by new editions, frequently incorporating a substantial part of the previous edition, the handbooks being edited and updated to stay abreast of the development in the technology they cover.

**9.33** Stock values for handbooks will have a similar composition to general publishers' titles, namely paper, printing costs, binding costs plus an oncost for overheads, but with the addition frequently of contributors' costs, and the accounting system of the publisher should analyse accumulating costs adequately for both accountant and auditor.

**9.34** The sales pattern tends to be spread over a period with the consequence that stocks of titles in publication tend to be larger in relation to sales than those for general publishers. Similar problems exist in assessing how many copies will be left unsold by the time that the next edition will be published, but, in view of the more steady demand over a period, projections of monthly sales levels are a firmer basis for the calculation of the write-down of stocks of any title.

**9.35** The audit checks indicated for general publishers will apply, with a changed emphasis to take account of the foregoing factors.

**9.36** Some publishers hold part of their stocks of handbooks in printed flat form, binding from such stocks as required to reduce the element of risk. Others will preserve their phototype setting to enable their editors to incorporate certain contributions in later editions. The latter are not usually valued as stock however and merely reduce the cost of a later edition. The printed flat stocks must be brought under the same review as for stocks for sale.

### Magazines and technical journals

**9.37** In the case of weekly and monthly magazines and technical journals there is a divergence of accounting method; some publishers choose to identify costs to each edition and others apportion costs on a time basis over a period. With either method of costing the question of values of stock for sale is of little relevance. Frequently, the accounts of such a publisher will incorporate say 12 or 52 publication dates to provide a realistic comparison year on year and to avoid problems of work-in-progress or stock valuation. Back numbers of earlier editions in stock are not usually valued.

**9.38** The problems which are encountered by the accountant and auditor relate not to stocks but to advertising revenue and payments to contributors for a series of articles. Advertising revenue is frequently received prior to publication in any event and where this spans an accounting date, consideration must be given to the provision for the transitory creditors, or debtors in the case of payments to contributors.

# TEXTILES

J. C. Bell

**Background to the business**

**10.01** The United Kingdom textile industry covers the range of manufacturing and merchanting activities from the preparation of fibres (both natural and synthetic) for conversion into yarns, through to the manufacture of clothing and household and industrial products from textile fabrics. This chapter is not concerned with the production of the raw fibre, but only with its preparation and conversion.

**10.02** The textile industry was one of the first to be organised on a factory basis during the Industrial Revolution and it developed rapidly during the latter part of the 19th century, aided by rapid world-wide economic and technological growth, improvements in transport and communications and the expansion of preferential markets in the developing British Empire. More recently, the growth of low wage-cost textile manufacturing industries in developing countries, especially in the Far East and Communist blocs, and technological innovation in the established textile industries of industrialised nations have contributed to the erosion of its competitive position.

**10.03** There are many manufacturing processes involved in conversion of raw fibre into a finished product for sale to the end user. Historically the industry has been fragmented, with specialised products and processes being carried out by independent producers. The formation of major combines at the turn of the 20th century principally involved horizontal mergers within sectors of the industry as did rationalisation during the 1930s depression. Also, following incentives provided by the Industry Reorganisation Acts of the early 1960s, further rationalisation ensued which was directed mainly at the elimination of surplus and obsolete capacity. However, the majority of larger mergers and acquisitions since the mid 1960s involved the development of vertically integrated businesses, which cover various stages of the production cycle from yarn spinning to distribution of finished products. Whilst traditionally, for climatic and geographical reasons, sections of the industry were concentrated in localised areas, the increased usage of synthetic and blended yarns, and the increasingly vertical structure of major producing groups, has tended to blur the previous geographical demarcations.

## Textile terminology

**10.04** The textile industry uses many time-honoured terms for its processes and products, although the trade vocabulary is regularly amended by the development of new types of production equipment and fabrics. It is important to have an understanding of textile manufacture to be familiar with the more commonly used terms and processes. The Textile Institute publishes a book entitled *Textile Terms and Definitions*, which provides a useful guide to terminology and basic manufacturing processes.

## Accounting problems

*Existence*

**10.05** To ascertain accurately textile stock quantities requires an orderly approach to stock recording and production control procedures, coupled with a well-organised approach to physical counting, recording and checking procedures. As in other manufacturing and merchanting businesses, careful control of cut-off procedures is required.

**10.06** Identification of yarn and fabric is not easy to the untrained eye, and it is therefore necessary for stocktakers to have sufficient technical knowledge to identify products and their quality, although the identity of the product, and the stage of production reached, should be evidenced by adequate process control documentation.

**10.07** In well-organised businesses, imperfect production will be identified and segregated for re-processing or disposal at various inspection points during the production process, but the stocktaking instructions should deal with the identification and recording at physical counting and also the procedures to be adopted by stocktakers to identify originally-acceptable production which may have deteriorated during handling or storage. It will normally be impractical to conduct a complete inspection of rolled or packed stocks and hence it will frequently be necessary to estimate the quantities of sub-standard product generation remaining undetected in normal production inspection procedure, based on recent customer rejection experience.

**10.08** Raw fibres and yarns are measured by weight, and natural fibres and yarns are susceptible to variations duc to moisture gains and losses from original trade tolerances arising during storage and processing. Quality-control procedures should be incorporated to ensure that any physical weights or measurements taken during physical stocktakings are adjusted for these variations.

**10.09** Many textile producers either sub-contract processing to other producers, or take in commission processing work themselves. It is important that both supplier and commission processor maintain accurate records of stocks given out to, and held on behalf of, third parties, as, without such records, the supplier cannot determine that all goods due are returned to him, nor can the processor verify his liability to the owner for any shortages.

**10.10** At physical stocktakings, all stocks on the producer's premises should be counted and reconciled with the producer's own and third-party stock records. Stocks balances held on behalf of third parties should be positively confirmed with the owners. Positive confirmation should also be obtained from third-party stockholders of all stock balances held to the producer's account. Any discrepancies should be fully reconciled, and provided for by the stockholder.

**10.11** Where stock held by third parties comprises a material part of a business's stocks, it is preferable that the owner's staff should attend to verify its existence physically. This can give rise to practical problems of access and administration, and the stockholder may hold indistinguishable stocks on his own or other processors' account, in which case reliance may have to be placed on the stockholder's certification of balances held.

**10.12** The most reliable approach to stocktaking is for a full physical inventory, during which production and movement of goods is stopped or carefully controlled, to be taken at the end of the accounting period. However, if the business has developed sufficiently reliable stock recording procedures which are regularly reconciled with and adjusted to periodic or rotational physical counts, it may prove acceptable to rely on book records of stock quantities for financial accounts purposes. This must be a matter of management judgement, based on the results of stock counts during the accounting period and an assessment of the proportion of total stock values physically verified within an acceptable interval prior to the accounting period end.

*Valuation*

**10.13** *Raw materials.* It will be appreciated that a variety of raw materials are used in the production of textile goods, both in terms of the fibres used in the manufacture of different types of yarn and cloth, and chemical and other additives used in the cleansing, colouring and finishing processes.

**10.14** Fibre and cloth are purchased either by contract from suppliers or on commodity markets in the United Kingdom or overseas; yarn and cloth producers frequently cover their forward purchase requirements and production by forward purchases and sales on the relevant future market, or by forward contracts with suppliers and customers.

**10.15** Natural fibre market prices can be subject to considerable volatility due to crop conditions and other supply and demand factors in international markets. Whilst a spot price is quoted on most textile commodity markets, there is frequently little spot trading in the commodity, the spot market being used principally for marginal deals in surplus or short stocks. A more reliable indication of a true market price may be found from forward market prices relating to a normal delivery cycle to manufacturers, or from the list prices of major merchants in the trade.

**10.16** Raw material stocks are normally valued at acquisition cost including duties, inward freight etc. In some businesses it is possible to identify the specific batches of raw materials held in raw materials' stocks, work-in-progress and finished goods, and hence to attribute actual cost prices to these materials. If identifiable materials were purchased to fulfil specific contracts, it is acceptable to value relevant stocks at actual cost, but stocks purchased for unspecified consumption should be valued on a FIFO or weighted average cost basis unless there is a specific justification for the consumption of raw materials other than in purchase sequence. It is considered that such situations are likely to arise only infrequently, probably in businesses producing goods with widely varying production and distribution cycles from the same raw material.

**10.17** Goods purchased in foreign currency are normally valued at the exchange rate ruling at the date of acquisition of title, unless the commitment is covered by forward purchase of currency or by a matching forward sale of the goods at a specified currency rate, in which case the forward contract rate should be used. Some variety of treatment of valuation of stocks purchased in foreign currency may be found in practice prior to the adoption of the United Kingdom Accounting Standard SSAP 20, 'Foreign currency translation'. Some businesses value such stocks at sterling settlement cost, or at period-end exchange rate if the stock had not been paid for at the end of the accounting period. The effect of these policies is to match exchange conversion differences with sales proceeds of the relevant stock, rather than including them in revenue on a time-related basis.

**10.18** The date of acquisition of title to stocks is not always readily apparent, particularly in the case of imported goods. Its determination requires knowledge of the rules of contract law and reference to the specific terms of individual purchase and shipping contracts.

**10.19** Whilst a commodity trader would normally provide for any net loss on uncovered open contracts, by reference to market price at the accounting date, a textile manufacturer or merchant convertor should take account of current market prices in calculating the net-realisable value of products into which raw material stocks are to be incorporated, but should only make a net-realisable value provision if a loss is foreseeable on sale of his ultimate product. In practice it may be difficult to predict the product into which a raw material is to be incorporated or the selling price at which the ultimate product is likely to be sold, and if experience indicates a close relationship between raw material market prices and product sale prices, particularly in the case of products with a high material content, it may be an acceptable accounting policy to value uncovered raw material stocks by reference to current market prices, if lower than cost, as a best estimate of net-realisable value.

**10.20** *Material content of work-in-progress and finished goods.* Material content of work-in-progress and finished goods should be determined by the development of reliable costing procedures which should be monitored against actual performance, and adjusted regularly to take account of price changes. Care must be taken to ensure that FIFO pricing of material content is related to supplies acquired immediately prior to the quantities included in raw material stocks.

**10.21** There is inherent wastage of material in most textile production processes, and a normal level of wastage and generation of imperfect product should be established. Finished products should be valued on the basis of the gross amount of raw material required to produce a normal level of acceptable product, net of anticipated recoveries from sale of waste and substandard production. Shrinkages and, less frequently, gains occur in most cloth printing and finishing processes; these are the subject of agreed tolerances between commission processors and their customers. The trade tolerance or the producer's own experience should be taken into account in calculating the finished product yield from underlying fabric.

**10.22** *Labour and overhead content of work-in-progress and finished goods.* The materiality of the labour and overhead element of the value of textile stocks and work-in-progress varies considerably between the production processes involved and type of fabric or garment produced. This factor should be considered when determining the type of costing system required to produce acceptably accurate stock valuations. More detailed allocation of variable and fixed production overheads to individual machine centres and products will be required in a mill carrying out a variety of processes on different products, using machinery with widely differing labour and overhead absorption characteristics, that will be necessary in a mill involved in standard production of a small product range.

**10.23** From 1980 to 1983 most sectors of the UK textile industry have suffered severe recession and many mills and factories have resorted to reduced shift or short-time working. During perids of volatile or depressed activity, care must be taken to ensure that process and product costings are amended to reflect a normal level of activity for the equipment concerned. Changes in unit costs arising from temporary fluctuations in level of trade should not be included in stock valuations, and should be charged against revenue of the period in which the abnormal production arose. However, where it is envisaged that a permanent change in production methods or staffing levels has taken place, the normal activity level should be re-appraised. This can frequently be a difficult judgement, particularly at times when the market is depressed or erratic.

**10.24** Normal SSAP 9 criteria apply to the nature of production overheads which should properly be included in textile stock valuations, although a pragmatic approach should be adopted in determining the extent to which design and pre-production marketing expenses should be included. The prudent approach is to charge such costs against revenue of the period in which they were incurred, unless the business has firm sales contracts or a sufficiently regular pattern of sales to justify spreading the expense over quantifiable product runs.

**10.25** Many textile products are fashion items sold in markets where design and colour changes can generate a significant level of obsolescence. Sales to multiple retailers and mail-order houses are frequently not subject to fixed volume contracts and producers may manufacture in excess of initial order quantities in the hope of repeat business which may not materialise, resulting in clearance sales at reduced prices in secondary markets. There is also a tendency during difficult trading conditions for a higher proportion of goods to be rejected by customers as being of sub-standard quality. Unless net-realisable values can be confirmed by post year-end sales contracts, it is necessary for the business's marketing management to make a detailed appraisal of anticipated proceeds in order to quantify the requirement for any net-realisable value provision.

**10.26** Consideration should be given to the valuation of substandard products identified during physical stocktaking and estimated as being inherent in stocks not subject to detailed inspection. Such goods should be valued at net-realisable value if less than cost, after deducting projected costs of uncompleted processing or rectification.

*Intra-group stock profits*

**10.27** In vertically structured textile businesses, products are frequently transferred between departments or subsidiaries at transfer prices reflecting a profit to the supplier. It is hence necessary to identify stocks to which processing has been applied by the group members, and to eliminate the element of unrealised profit and administration and finance overheads in order to re-state stocks at prices at which they would have been valued by the supplying unit.

**Auditing problems**

*General considerations*

**10.28** In the main, the problems arising in the audit of textile stocks are common to the majority of manufacturing businesses. Matters affecting auditors' attendance at stocktaking (including rotational stock-counts) are described in Statement 3.902 (U9) of the ICAEW *Members' Handbook* and other matters relating to the audit of stocks and work-in-progress are dealt with in Statement 3.903 (U11). Auditors can draw guidance on the general principles of stock valuation and reporting requirements in financial statements from SSAP 9 (*Stocks and Work-in-Progress*), and the audit approach should be determined along the principles set out in *Auditing Standards and Guidelines*.

**10.29** Apart from general auditing and financial reporting principles, the auditor's main concern in the audit of textile stocks is likely to relate to the accounting problems which commonly arise in textile-stock valuation which are referred to in the preceding sections of this chapter, and reference is made to particular matters giving rise to difficulties to auditors below.

*Physical existence and title to stocks*

**10.30** The principal problem confronting an auditor of textile stocks is to gain an understanding of the terminology of the textile industry and the manufacturing processes involved. It is unlikely that an auditor will be sufficiently expert in textile technology to be able to identify particular yarn and fabric types, or the stage of production reached by work-in-progress, but he should be able to draw audit evidence as to the correctness of product descriptions and quantities established at physical stocktakings, from his review of the adequacy of internal controls applied in the stocktaking procedures, and from stock records and production-control documentation relating to the goods concerned. The auditor should use his knowledge of the weighing and measuring techniques available, and their reliability, in order to form an opinion on the accuracy of the methods used to establish quantities of particular products, and he should be able to draw additional audit evidence from observation of the stocktaking and from his own test counting.

**10.31** Particular care is required in the case of producers who also commission-process or otherwise hold stocks on behalf of third parties. All third-party stocks should be counted at the client's physical stocktakings, and should be agreed with third-party stock records. The auditor should also ensure that third-party stocks are not included in the client's own stock valuation. Where the amounts of third-party stocks held by the client are material, the auditor should obtain direct confirmation from the owner of the stock balances held to the owner's account. Conversely, where material quantities of the client's stock are held by third parties, the auditor should obtain direct confirmation from the custodian of the balances held, and should also examine reports of any periodic inspections of the stock by the client's own employees and should make enquiries as to the standing of the custodian where circumstances warrant it.

*Stock valuation*

**10.32** The auditor's problems in verifying costing procedures and stock valuations will vary considerably depending on the nature and variety of processes undertaken, and the degree of sophistication of the client's costing procedures. However, if material costs are incorporated at average or standard prices, the auditor must ensure that the client's procedures for re-statement to actual cost on a FIFO basis of materials cost are materially accurate, particularly where price-volatile commodities are involved. The auditor should also review the information necessary to support the accuracy of wastage and weight or length gain or loss factors incorporated into costings.

**10.33** The auditor must form a judgement on the assumptions made by the client in assessing normal levels of activity for production overhead recovery purposes. These would normally be based on current operating levels and shift working patterns, but should have regard to a reasonably efficient level of production so that the effect of temporary fluctuations is eliminated. The reason for any change from a previously established level should be ascertained and confirmed, and if the effect is material, consideration should be given to quantifying the effect in a note to the financial statements.

*Obsolescence and net-realisable value*

**10.34** The auditor should ensure that the client has applied appropriate procedures to identify defective, slow-moving and obsolete stocks through physical stocktaking procedures, review of stock movements and levels, and correlation with forward sales orders and forecasts. Obsolescence is likely to be most frequent in stocks which are subject to rapid changes in fashion or seasonal sales patterns.

**10.35** Unless covered by post year-end sales or orders, assessment of the net-realisable value of stocks will require judgement by the client's marketing staff based on prudent estimates of prices attainable in the markets in which the goods are expected to be sold, at the time when they will be available for sale, and should take account of projected costs of completion and distribution.

**10.36** In depressed markets or times of rapidly changing raw material prices, contracts may have been taken at net-realisable values below production cost. The auditor should review unexecuted sales orders in order to identify any loss-making items.

**10.37** The auditor should review the utilisation of prior year obsolescence and net-realisable value provisions as an aid to assessment of the reliability of the client's judgements.

# SOLICITORS AND OTHER PROFESSIONALS

D. W. Davis

### Introduction

**11.01** Although this chapter is written specifically with solicitors in mind, it applies in general terms to all professional practices.

**11.02** The general principles of work-in-progress valuation apply as much to the valuation of work-in-progress of a solicitor or other professional as to any other business. Wide variations in practice exist, however, because there is no statutory obligation on a solicitor, as there is on a company under the Companies Act 1948, to draw up his accounts so as to show a true and fair view of his state of affairs and of his profit or loss.

**11.03** Whether a solicitor's accounts must show a true and fair view is decided upon in the course of discussions between the solicitor and his accountant. In the case of partnerships, the question may be covered by the partnership agreement or by discussion between the partners. Allied to this question is the form that the accountant's report upon the accounts should take. Where it is intended that the accounts should give a true and fair view, they must be prepared on the basis of a full work-in-progress valuation to comply with the requirements of SSAP 9. This statement of course applies not only to incorporated businesses, but to any business whose accounts are intended to show a true and fair view.

**11.04** However, if there is no requirement for a true and fair view, the alternative bases for valuing work-in-progress can be considered. Their respective merits should be reviewed in any case from time to time to see whether a departure from the true and fair view is advantageous.

**11.05** That such wide variations can exist in the basis of valuation of work-in-progress is related to the indulgent attitude of the Inland Revenue, who in looking at a solicitor's accounts for tax purposes seeks the assurance of consistency of method of valuation rather than of the propriety of the method applied. Several bases of valuation therefore have general acceptance and apply to sole practitioners and partnerships alike.

**Lower of cost and net-realisable value**

**11.06** For a proper measure of practice profitability and performance, the preferred basis for valuation of work-in-progress must be that which accords with generally accepted accounting principles. This basis is the lower of cost and net-realisable value. The majority of solicitors value their work-in-progress on this basis, but the size of the majority is not large and the basis is more prevalent amongst the larger firms than the smaller firms or sole practitioners.

**11.07** This method of valuation involves bringing into the valuation each item of unbilled work at its actual cost or at its realisable value, if lower. The valuation commences with the ascertainment of every item of unbilled work, usually from time records. The time records should show for every client the time occupied by every grade of staff and partner. The time records may be written-up manually or on a computerised system, so that this will show not only the time spent but either the evaluated cost of this time or the evaluated value at charging rates from which cost can be calculated. Occasionally the source of information will be diary entries where this is the chosen method of time recording.

**11.08** Actual cost of work-in-progress covers a number of elements:

(a) the salary cost of the staff employed and sometimes the notional salary cost of the principal(s) engaged on the work;

(b) the proportionate overhead cost attributable to the work performed;

(c) disbursements; and

(d) a deduction for part-billings or billings-on-account.

**11.09** The salary cost will be easily ascertainable, though costs such as employer's national insurance contributions and pension costs should not be overlooked. There is no obligation (certainly not for tax purposes) to value partners' time, but sometimes for management information purposes a notional salary cost is placed upon each principal's work. This gives a more meaningful value to work-in-progress at any time and from year to year.

**11.10** The applicable overhead costs are all those which contribute to the performance of work for clients and they generally comprise all those expenses of the practice other than salary costs. The only outgoings from a solicitor's practice not likely to be included in his work-in-progress valuation are drawings or capital payments such as payments for goodwill and fixed assets.

**11.11** Selling costs are an overhead which should not be included in a work-in-progress valuation, but a solicitor's practice will not be incurring costs of this nature to any significant extent. In the case of other professional practices, however, these costs should be excluded from the overheads brought into the work-in-progress valuation.

**11.12** As with manufacturers, overheads should be added into work-in-progress by reference to the normal level of activity. If for any reason the practice has been working below this level, the proportion of overheads attributable to the shortfall in activity should be excluded. Solicitors are usually well able to adapt their practices to suit their level of work and often there is a buffer of work in hand to smooth matters along. On the other hand, if not all of a solicitor's staff are fully engaged on client work, i.e. if they are working below their capacity, then the effect on overheads must be eliminated from the valuation.

**11.13** Disbursements to be included should be all those recoverable expenses paid out on behalf of clients and not already recovered from them at the valuation date. Non-recoverable expenses should be included as overheads.

**11.14** If part of the work being valued has been brought into earnings by part-billing, that part should be eliminated, just as work relating to a final bill or invoice would be eliminated. The part-billing is at selling price, whereas the amount to be eliminated is the cost of the work billed. Sometimes part-billings are called billings- or payments-on-account.

**11.15** However, where billings-on-account are not brought into earnings, but are merely a means of accelerating cash collections, then the whole of the payments (but excluding value added tax) that have not been covered by subsequent final bills should be deducted from the work-in-progress valuation.

**11.16** The sum of all the elements of cost may be compounded into valuation rates for each staff member and partner, taking into account the total actual chargeable hours of each staff member and partner during the accounting period. Where the actual chargeable hours cannot be readily computed, they should be estimated.

**11.17** When chargeable hours are restricted by administrative tasks for the practice, the proportion of salary cost relating to these administrative tasks should be included as an overhead.

**11.18** The computation of valuation rates might proceed on the basis of the following example, where the applicable overheads amount to £25,000.

| | *Chargeable hours per annum* | *Salary cost per annum* | *Salary cost plus overheads per annum* | *Valuation rate per hour* |
|---|---|---|---|---|
| Partner | 1,400 | £12,000 | £23,111 | £16.50 |
| Staff member A | 1,540 | £9,000 | £17,333 | £11.25 |
| Staff member B | 1,600 | £6,000 | £11,556 | £7.22 |
| | | £27,000 | £52,000 | |

**11.19** The valuation rate excludes any profit element so that the relevant charging rates would be at least 30 per cent higher, often 50 per cent higher and sometimes 100 per cent higher or more.

**11.20** The respective valuation rates applied to the time incurred at the various grades give the valuation of the time. To this must be added the total of recoverable disbursements with the part-billings deducted to give the net work-in-progress valuation.

**11.21** As before, a valuation of partners' time is made only for management purposes and would not be included in the valuation of work-in-progress made for tax purposes.

**11.22** The valuations produced on the above basis should be carefully reviewed to confirm that they are recoverable in due course from clients. Often they are not because solicitors tend to charge fees not merely based on the value of work performed but also upon the means of the client. An extreme example of this is work upon a trust set up many years ago where the proper fee for the solicitor's work alone, because of inflation, now far exceeds the total trust-fund income. There may be other cases where the solicitor feels indulgent towards his client.

**11.23** Where the estimated fee does not cover all applicable costs, the appropriate valuation is the lower of:

(a) the proportionate part of the estimated fee related to the work performed; and

(b) the fee or estimated fee less the cost at valuation rates of completing the work.

**11.24** Where contingencies in relation to items of uncompleted work are not capable of being estimated, then the work is best omitted from the valuation.

**11.25** It may also be that work-in-progress is not realisable because the client is without funds. A review of work-in-progress needs to be undertaken to exclude that relating to doubtful payers. The debts for which provisions for bad and doubtful debts have been made, will have some bearing on this question.

**11.26** Where a fixed or scale fee applies, the valuation should be the lower of:

(a) the cost of the work performed as calculated above;

(b) the proportionate part of the fixed or estimated scale fee related to the work performed; and

(c) the fixed fee or estimated scale fee less the cost at valuation rates of completing the work.

**11.27** Most practices now keep time records and often these are computerised using a bureau or an in-house computer. Because of the decrease in real terms of the cost of mini or micro computers, all but the smallest practices can now afford in-house computers to deal not only with their fee ledgers and other applications but also with their time ledgers. Clearly, the chore of making useful work-in-progress valuations is much reduced by this process.

**11.28** The prices used for costing work-in-progress on a computerised system (and sometimes on a manual system) are usually the charging rates. Where time costs as distinct from valuations at charging rates are not available from the computer system, the total valuation at charging rates may be reduced by a simple factor to eliminate the profit mark-up. The factor should be based on immediate past performance and upon current budgets and charging rate calculations. Care with this calculation should be taken to ensure that the current impact of inflation upon a practice is correctly interpreted.

**Valuations for tax purposes**

*The possibilities*

**11.29** Provided that the professional practice is consistent in its accounting approach, the Inland Revenue will accept the following bases of accounting for determining profits:

(a) Cash basis of accounting (excluding all work-in-progress and debtors). This basis is sometimes called the conventional basis;

(b) Bills delivered basis (including debtors but excluding work-in-progress). This basis is also sometimes referred to as the conventional basis or partial basis;

(c) Full work-in-progress basis (including debtors). This is the accruals or earnings basis.

*The cash basis*

**11.30** By this basis, a solicitor brings into account only cash received and he excludes therefore any recognition of bills delivered but not yet paid for and excludes any work-in-progress valuation. The solicitor would also exclude creditors and accrued charges, though the amount of these will be small compared to debtors and work-in-progress, or even compared to debtors alone. There are clear benefits to tax assessments and to cash flow from this basis because the increments by which work-in-progress and debtors grow year by year, not merely due to expansion of the practice but also to ever present inflation, are excluded from the tax assessments. The exclusion from the tax assessments is merely a deferral to later years, but it is a deferral which perpetuates and grows year by year. The eventual benefit can therefore be enormous.

**11.31** There are benefits too in calculating the profits in this way from the effect it has upon cash outflow in the restriction of drawings. If prudence appeals, the solicitor may thus keep his drawings down to the profits actually collected in cash. For a practice that allows its work-in-progress or its debtors to be at too high a level, this is a good discipline.

**11.32** There are disadvantages too, of course; these are considered below.

**11.33** Because of the distorted way in which this basis can present profits, the Inland Revenue will not accept it for the three accounting years after the commencement of a practice. Nevertheless, once this initial period is past, a change to the cash basis (or bills delivered basis) should be carefully considered. This may be advantageous, even though double taxation of some items appears to result as cash received is brought into income for a second time following the change, having been brought in in a previous period on the earnings basis.

**11.34** If a change to the cash basis is decided upon, it is an additional advantage to maximise cash collections in the year before the change; a distinct benefit arises!

*Bills delivered basis*

**11.35** On this basis, a solicitor brings into account only those bills raised by the time of the accounting date. While the possible tax deferment is not as great as under the cash basis, the bills delivered basis still offers a deferment for bills not raised for uncompleted work. Because of the obvious manipulation of results from year to year that can be performed, the Inland Revenue sometimes requests from a solicitor applying this basis an undertaking that bills will not be delayed for taxation purposes. There are still planning advantages, however, in deferring profits from a good year to an ensuing poor year, as it is never within the remit of the Inland Revenue to insist on an undertaking that work is completed promptly!

**11.36** Often a solicitor's accounts include a fixed valuation for work-in-progress as agreed with the Inland Revenue; sometimes this is increased on an *ad hoc* basis, again by agreement with the Inland Revenue. These valuations usually bear no relationship to the true value of work-in-progress and in practice this basis is similar to the bills delivered basis.

**11.37** Again the disadvantages of the bills delivered basis must be carefully considered.

*Full work-in-progress basis*

**11.38** The valuation of work-in-progress at the lower of cost and net-realisable value (the full work-in-progress valuation) is the basis generally accepted by the Inland Revenue, but a solicitor may still exclude from the valuation any value for his own time, since remuneration for that time is not an expense of the partnership.

**11.39** As before, a valuation basis excluding even only partners' time, may be disadvantageous for other reasons as described below.

## Disadvantages of special bases other than full work-in-progress basis

*Measuring profitability*

**11.40** It cannot be stressed too strongly that a solicitor needs, as do all businessmen, a reliable barometer of the profitability of his practice over a succession of accounting periods, whether they be monthly, quarterly or yearly. For this purpose he needs to base his periodic accounts on a sound valuation of work-in-progress and debtors; this valuation should be at the lower of cost and net-realisable value. Failing this, a valuation at selling price would be a useful alternative.

**11.41** It matters not which is the chosen method of valuation for tax purposes as it is a simple adjustment (and not an unusual practice) to alter the management accounts at the annual accounting date, if prepared on a full work-in-progress basis, in order to present the profit on the basis chosen for tax purposes.

**11.42** An economy in the cost of computing the work-in-progress valuation may be a false economy indeed where the cheaper valuation, not involving a 'full work-in-progress valuation', misleads the solicitor as to the comparative profitability of his practice year by year. As a result, he may set inadequate charging rates which have no regard to the requirement to maintain capital and earnings.

*Changes in partners or in partners' profit shares*

**11.43** A second disadvantage of any basis of valuation other than a 'full work-in-progress valuation' is that it may lead to an inequitable distribution of profits between partners when profit shares are changed between one year and the next, or when a partner is admitted or retires. This is a situation which partners often fail to consider or to understand.

**11.44** An example emphasises this point. Consider a firm with partners A, B and C. They share profits 50 per cent, 40 per cent and 10 per cent respectively. At the end of year 5, the profit-sharing ratio changes to equality. For simplicity, changes in debtors and creditors are ignored. Profit and loss accounts prepared on the full work-in-progress valuation basis compared to the cash basis are as follows:

**Example**

*Profit and loss account – Year 5*

| | *'Full work-in-progress valuation' basis* | *Cash basis* |
|---|---|---|
| | £ | £ |
| Fees received | 100,000 | 100,000 |
| Increase in work-in-progress | 20,000 | — |
| Cash payments for salaries and expenses | (60,000) | (60,000) |
| Profit for year before taxation | £60,000 | £40,000 |
| Partner C's share – 10 per cent | £6,000 | £4,000 |

*Profit and loss account – Year 6*

| | | |
|---|---|---|
| Fees received | 152,000 | 152,000 |
| Decrease in work-in-progress | (20,000) | — |
| Cash payments for salaries and expenses | (65,000) | (65,000) |
| Profit for year before taxation | £67,000 | £87,000 |
| Partner C's share – 33⅓ per cent | £22,333 | £29,000 |
| Partner C's share for Year 5 and Year 6 | £28,333 | £33,000 |

**11.45** In year 5, work-in-progress has accumulated at the expense of billings and collections. The trend is reversed in year 6. In this situation, partners increasing their shares at the end of year 5 benefit to the detriment of partners whose shares have decreased.

**11.46** The partners should be aware of the implications of their accounting basis upon their respective profit shares and may wish to adjust any capital payments being made between the partners upon changes in the partners or in their profit shares.

*Post-cessation receipts*

**11.47** It has already been said that a beneficial tax basis is only a deferment of taxation. The moment of reckoning comes under Section 144, Income and Corporation Taxes Act 1970, coupled with Sections 137, 138 and 143, whereby, after the discontinuance of a practice, post-cessation receipts of amounts not already brought into account for any period are assessed under Sch. D, Case VI. The amounts involved can be substantial especially where the cash basis has been applied.

**11.48** The discontinuance might arise upon the retirement of the solicitor (who was a sole practitioner), a deemed discontinuance upon a change in partners where they do not elect for a continuing basis of assessment, or upon the merger of one practice into another which has used some other basis of valuation.

The prospect, however, of post-cessation assessments does not necessarily detract from the cash-flow benefits which derive from a conventional basis, even though the effects, in due course, of Section 144 should be borne in mind.

## Stock relief

**11.49** The introduction of stock relief in 1973/74 for increases in professional work-in-progress made the advantages of the conventional basis less clear. Of course, if work-in-progress was not valued at all, as on the conventional basis, there could be no stock relief. Where the earnings basis applied, however, an allowance was given for an increase in work-in-progress, making the increase free of taxation.

**11.50** Under the scheme of stock relief which has applied from 14 November 1980, the tax relief given is on a notional increase calculated by reference to the opening work-in-progress valuation, less a deduction of £2,000. This increase is that shown by the movement in the all-stocks index for the accounting year. An up-to-date list of movements in the index is published every month. If the effect of the tax relief for increases in work-in-progress, as calculated by the stock index, is largely to eliminate all profits arising from increases in work-in-progress, there is little benefit in adopting the conventional basis.

**11.51** For a solicitor with an expanding practice, however, the stock-relief scheme seems unlikely to give him relief for work-in-progress increases attributable to volume changes, as well as for increases attributable to price changes alone. In these circumstances, the merits of the conventional basis still require attention and it may well be preferable to adopt the conventional basis.

## Audit considerations

*General*

**11.52** Solicitors vary in their desire to have their accounts audited and of course there is no mandatory audit requirement. Where an audit is required, it is basically for the solicitor or the partnership agreement to specify the terms of the engagement. It is desirable for the auditor to discuss the terms of the engagement with the solicitor to ensure that the desired services, and no more than these, are being given. Sometimes an audit is not required and an accountant's report, as distinct from an auditor's report, will suffice.

*True and fair view*

**11.53** It is usually in the context that the accounts are to give a true and fair view that an audit opinion is required. As mentioned previously, a true and fair view is obtained only by use of a 'full work-in-progress valuation'. If a conventional basis is used, the auditor should express his opinion appropriately and should not refer in his opinion to a true and fair view. Indeed, in these circumstances it is probably best to avoid use of the term 'audit' and for the accountant to give instead an accountant's report rather than an auditor's report. In addition, it will generally be helpful to describe the accounting basis being used in the notes to the accounts.

**11.54** Where the solicitor does not require an audit opinion on his accounts but where the 'full work-in-progress valuation' basis is used, the accountant preparing and reporting on the accounts should consider his position carefully. Although an audit opinion is not being given, the accountant will want his accounts to be reliable. In these circumstances, his tests will be similar in nature to those of the auditor, even though the extent of the tests may differ.

*Procedures*

**11.55** Assuming that the solicitor uses the 'full work-in-progress valuation' and that an audit opinion is to be given on the accounts incorporating this valuation, the auditor should adopt a normal programme of audit work for verifying work-in-progress. The audit programme should, however, include the following matters.

**11.56** There will be no annual stocktake to attend, but the need for verification of the existence of the work-in-progress and of the extent to which the work is complete should be considered. The testing of existence may hardly be necessary in a small partnership, but where a larger number of staff are employed by the solicitor, it will be necessary to examine work records to confirm:

(a) that work-in-progress is properly supported by time records;

(b) that all work-in-progress is listed;

(c) that the stage of completion of the work-in-progress is properly estimated.

**11.57** The valuation of the work-in-progress will be primarily by reference to time occupied, as described in paragraph 11.16, but examination of the stage completed is necessary where a fixed or scale fee is to be charged (see paragraph 11.26). In such cases, the auditor will wish to see that the evaluated time in excess of that recoverable has been excluded from the valuation.

**11.58** The auditor should carry out a review of the realisability of work-in-progress. This work should be carried out in conjunction with the examination of the provisions for bad and doubtful debtors, as the list of clients covered by the work-in-progress valuation may include clients who are already debtors. The auditor should ensure that all large values of work for individual clients are included in his review, as well as work which is being slow to be completed.

**Conclusion**

**11.59** Valuation of a solicitor's work-in-progress gives little practical difficulty, provided loss-making work is carefully segregated. By contrast, consideration of the taxation effects is complex and involved, and circumstances change as does tax legislation. While a full work-in-progress valuation gives more meaningful accounts, there may be reasons for not adopting this basis for taxation. The fuller the understanding of the solicitor or his partners of the taxation consequences, the greater is his satisfaction likely to be with the choice of valuation basis.

**11.60** Once tax assessments are on a full earnings basis, probably the solicitor is best off in the long term to stay on this basis. Where continued expansions of the practice seem likely, however, a change to the conventional basis may be advantageous.

**11.61** Where a conventional basis applies, however, there may in some cases be an advantage in changing to an earnings basis and obtaining stock relief. However, the cost in tax of a change to the earnings basis in terms of accelerated cash outflow may be considerable. Only a careful examination of the circumstances can reveal the best approach.

# BOOKSHOPS

## R. J. Fox

**Background to bookselling in the UK**

**12.01** There are around 3,300 stockholding bookshops in the UK, which sell new books with a great range in respect of size, type of goods sold and accounting systems. At one end of the scale there is the sole trader, an expert bookseller, running a small bookshop and perhaps specialising in, for example, historical or religious books. At the other extreme is the high-street multiple, concentrating on popular and standard texts and with its sophisticated, but impersonal, selling and financial procedures.

**12.02** Bookselling is a seasonal business. The demand for academic text-books peaks in September and October and for general books in the weeks leading up to Christmas. Once the New Year Sales are over, the remainder of the first six months of the calendar year is less busy.

**12.03** As one might imagine, there is a high degree of interdependence between individual booksellers and publishers. This is reflected at an official level where there is regular co-operation between the Booksellers Association and the Publishers Association.

**Special features of bookselling**

**12.04** Before discussing the stock valuation problems of bookshops, it is necessary to have a basic understanding of some of the special features of bookselling.

*Net book agreement*

**12.05** Bookselling is one of the few trades where resale price maintenance is still in force. The Net Book Agreement, administered by the Publishers Association, is designed to prevent price cutting among booksellers which could result in, amongst other things, poorer service to the consumer and the demise of many booksellers.

**12.06** All British published books fall into two categories, 'net' and 'non-net'. Books classified as net comprise the majority of books sold in general bookshops. These books have the price printed on the cover or jacket and, generally speaking, must not be sold at less than the printed price (unless they are damaged or more than 12 months old, and have been offered back to the publisher). These prices are legally enforceable by the publisher under the terms of the Net Book Agreement. The fact that a book is a 'net book' will always be indicated on the invoice rendered by the publisher, as this shows the published price as well as the cost price to the bookseller. The difference between the selling and cost prices, the discount, is negotiable between the publisher and the bookseller.

**12.07** The other category, non-net books, are not subject to the Net Book Agreement and can therefore be sold at any price decided by the bookseller. These books are invariably school text books, bibles and hymn books which are to be sold in bulk quantities to educational or religious organisations, and are not normally to be found in any great quantity in a normal stockholding retail bookshop. Bookshops with school customers may keep a few copies of the more usual books known to be in use in their locality and usually sell single copies at a higher price.

**12.08** There are two main instances when a net book can be offered at a discount:

(a) Bookshops can participate in the annual National Book Sale which is well publicised in the media and takes place usually over a 10-day period, in January or February. For this they can mark down books which they have held for more than 12 months, and in addition can buy in special sale stock from publishers;

(b) Bookshops can sell net books at a discount to certain authorised institutions such as public libraries.

*Returns*

**12.09** The ability to send back surplus goods to suppliers is another unusual feature of the book trade. Conditions vary between publishers but provided:

(a) the stock is not old or damaged; and

(b) the publisher's permission is obtained in advance (unless the publisher supplied incorrect or damaged books etc.),

the bookseller can often return most surplus stock and usually obtain full credit. Each publisher's conditions are summarised in the *Directory of British Publishers and Their Terms* which is published annually by the Booksellers Association. The extent to which booksellers can return books often depends on their financial muscle. A large chain of book stores is likely to be more successful, therefore, at returning surplus stock than a small independent shop, since publishers are inclined only to accept multiple copies as returns rather than singles. The success of the small bookshop will depend more on the rapport with the publishers. Returns to publishers are usually recorded on the Booksellers Association standard returns forms.

*Margin analysis*

**12.10** Publishers' discounts vary enormously over the different categories of goods sold in a typical bookshop. A rough guide is as follows:

| | |
|---|---|
| Stationery and greetings cards | over 35 per cent |
| General hardback and paperback books (net) | 30 per cent–35 per cent |
| Academic books (net) | 25 per cent–33 per cent |

'Net books' are sold to public libraries at a discount of around 10 per cent if the library possesses a library licence from the Publishers Association.

On 'non-net' books the booksellers usually receive $17\frac{1}{2}$ per cent from publishers and may give a discount to the school/authority of up to $12\frac{1}{2}$ per cent.

**12.11** A typical bookseller will have difficulty in achieving a gross margin over 30 per cent owing to surcharges on small orders, carriage costs and very low publishers' discounts on non-net school books.

**12.12** The extent to which bookshops analyse their trading accounts varies considerably. Most shops only analyse their trading accounts between VATable items, for example stationery and greetings cards and non-VATable items, i.e. all books. What the accountant or auditor looks for is a further analysis of the trading account over the main categories of books, for example general hardbacks, paperbacks, retail academic, library supplies and local authority contracts. Although most shops could analyse their sales over these headings, they could not cope with analysing their purchase invoices and provision for returns over the same headings. Furthermore, some shops do not have proper procedures for recording the values of books which are transferred from 'good stock' to be sold at a reduced price or at a discount.

This inability to analyse gross margins is a severe drawback when reviewing the reasonability of the stock figure in the annual accounts. In assessing the overall gross margin, allowance needs to be made for the following factors:

(a) books sold at a reduced price during the National Book Sale and special remaindered stock purchased from publishers;

(b) pilferage, which cannot be quantified precisely, but may be anything between 1 per cent–3 per cent of sales;

(c) changes in the frequency and size of purchase orders, as this will affect the discount given by publishers.

**12.13** The Charter Group of the Booksellers Association in conjunction with the Manchester Business School, produces an annual Economic Survey. This inter-firm publication contains a wealth of financial and statistical information on the sales and profitability of shops by size of outlet, specialisation etc. Used properly by the bookseller and his accountant, this publication will help to identify those parts of the business where an improvement in profitability, for example stock turn, could be achieved.

*Stock levels and records*

**12.14** The high degree to which a bookseller needs to know his stock is another important feature of the industry. A successful bookseller may have well over 1,000 titles in stock and yet will not only know if a particular book is in stock but precisely where it can be found on the shelf.

**12.15** Besides being able to exercise this custodial control over his physical stock, the bookseller is likely to maintain a stockcard for each title in stock, probably using the standard stock-control card of the Booksellers Association, a copy of which is reproduced opposite:

**12.16** The cards are usually filed in title sequence, by publisher, for each section of the shop. This sequence enables the bookseller to carry out a detailed review of all stock usually at least once a month and, in addition, to check quickly a particular publisher's stock prior to a representative's visit.

**12.17** These cards, however, are kept principally for ordering purposes. They are of limited use to the auditor, firstly because they are not integrated with the accounting records and secondly, there is usually a broken audit trail when trying to confirm conclusively, for example, during the audit of purchases, that a particular book is still in stock, or has been sold or returned.

**12.18** The bookseller will be well aware of the need to minimise his investment in stocks and will refer to the Economic Survey to compare his stock turn with the averages achieved by similar shops.

**STOCK CONTROL CARD – DO NOT REMOVE**

| AUTHOR: | | | | | | | PUBLISHER: | | | | |
|---|---|---|---|---|---|---|---|---|---|---|---|
| TITLE: | | | | | | | | | I.S.B.N. | | |
| PUB. CATEGORY | | | REORDER LEVEL | | | | MAX. STOCK: | | | PRICE: | |
| T.V. | FILM | RADIO | O.U. | G.C.E. | C.S.E. | SECTION: | | | | | |
| DATE | STOCK | Quantity ordered | DATE ordered (or O. No.) | DATE received (or Report) | SALES | DATE | STOCK | Quantity ordered | DATE ordered (or O. No.) | DATE received (or Report) | SALES |
| | | | | | | | | | | | |
| | | | | | | | | | | | |
| | | | | | | | | | | | |
| | | | | | | | | | | | |
| | | | | | | | | | | | |
| | | | | | | | | | | | |
| | | | | | | | | | | | |
| | | | | | | | | | | | |
| | | | | | | | | | | | |
| | | | | | | | | | | | |

*Teleordering*

**12.19** To try to combat increases in postal charges and postal delays, an increasing number of publishers and bookshops have joined the Teleordering Scheme. Under this arrangement, the bookseller orders books by using a computer terminal in his shop. Overnight the Teleordering central computer automatically calls up the orders from each bookshop. The orders are then sorted into publisher sequence and consolidated orders are transmitted by the central computer to each publisher. An order confirmation is transmitted back to the bookshop and a hard copy can be printed the following day.

*Book tokens*

**12.20** The accountant or auditor will need to understand how book tokens are controlled and taken into the accounts. The bookseller accounts to Book Tokens Limited on a quarterly basis, either receiving or paying the difference between tokens sold and tokens received. If he has exchanged more tokens than he has sold, Book Tokens Limited will send him a cheque for the difference less $12\frac{1}{2}$ per cent commission. If he has sold more tokens than he has exchanged, he pays the difference less $12\frac{1}{2}$ per cent.

*International standard book number (ISBN)*

**12.21** The purpose of the ISBN is to give each title a unique identifying number. The ISBN, which is printed on the cover of the book and on the verso of the title page, is the key reference number used by booksellers, librarians and publishers when communicating about books and it is around this number that the Teleordering Scheme functions.

The Publishers Association and the Booksellers Association have recently published *Machine Readable Codes for the Book Trade.* This operating manual specifies how the ISBN is to appear on the back cover of books in a machine-readable form, thus enabling it to be captured by electronic means for computer processing. The summary has this to say on the benefits to the trade. 'Reading devices at the point-of-sale will enable booksellers to record each book sold. More sophisticated point-of-sale systems can perform stock control and sales analysis functions simultaneously. An assistant will be able to pass a light pen or wand over the symbol on the book itself, or pass a book over a fixed scanning beam. The ISBN which is read could be compared with the stock records held by a minicomputer. The price could be abstracted from the database, the stock record adjusted, the sale item logged and the price, description and/or ISBN shown on the cash till and printed on the receipt which could then be given to the customer.'

An accountant or auditor is well placed to help the bookseller seize the opportunities of computerisation.

**Stocktaking**

**12.22** Stocktaking at a bookshop is a tedious job as it involves listing a large number of low value items. A traditional bookshop is a bit of a rabbit warren and it is essential that a detailed plan of each floor is prepared before the stocktake. Each shelf in the selling area should be identified on the plan and numbered, and the plan should also show other points in the building where stock is held, for example in the shop windows, and in the storeroom, offices etc.

**12.23** Each book shows the selling price. The price of 'net' books will be printed on the cover and the bookseller will have pencilled the selling price of 'non-net' books on the inside of the cover. Stock is therefore counted at selling price. Two people are usually involved; one person calling out the selling price and the other entering this on an add listing machine. The tape totals for each shelf should be recorded on the stock summary which should be cross-referenced to the shelf numbers on the plan. Some booksellers borrow the add listing machines for the physical stockcount and errors are likely if the assistants are unfamiliar with the machines. The most common error is to fail to clear machines at the end of each run.

**12.24** The bookseller may consider reducing the time taken to count paperbacks by adopting an old practice used by some large shops, in which the shelf footage occupied by paperbacks is measured and multiplied by the average price per foot. However, this technique should be discouraged as nowadays the price of individual paperbacks varies widely.

**12.25** The bookseller will need an adequate system for controlling the receipt of books from publishers. In most instances the invoice arrives with the books. Most booksellers keep a simple 'gatebook' showing date, publisher's name, publisher's invoice number and the number of parcels received. It is impracticable to list in the 'gatebook' the actual books received. Therefore, once the boxes are unpacked and the books placed on the shelves, it is time-consuming (and impossible in the case of popular books which are ordered frequently) to trace specific books on the shelves via the gatebook to invoices. The auditor therefore needs to examine cut-off when attending the stockcount, to ensure that there is a system for marking purchase invoices and returns notes pre-stock and post-stock.

**Cut-off and returns**

**12.26** The bookseller should be aware of the following points on cut-off:

(a) Books received prior to their advertised publication date should be omitted from stock and creditors;

(b) Customers' deposits in respect of unfulfilled orders, and books awaiting collection by customers (against which a deposit may or may not have been received) need to be accounted for properly;

(c) The balance with Book Tokens Limited will need to be calculated if the bookseller's year-end does not correspond with the date of the quarterly return to Book Tokens Limited.

**12.27** As far as the larger booksellers are concerned, the whole area of purchases/stock cut-off is a headache. Reconciling suppliers' statements with purchase ledgers often presents a major problem, due to a combination of the following factors:

(a) Many large publishers have a computerised sales ledger, whereby the despatch/invoice documentation is generated when the bookseller's order is input to the computer. Because of delays at the publisher and/or postal delays, there may be a gap of up to three or four weeks between the date of the invoice on the publisher's statement and the date that the goods are received by the bookseller. If the bookseller has branches, and if goods and invoices are delivered direct to the branches, there may be a longer time delay before the invoice, duly approved, is received at the bookseller's central accounts department. When reconciling statements, therefore, there may be many recent invoices shown on the statements about which the bookseller knows nothing. If the bookseller's goods inward procedures are inadequate, the bookseller and/or auditor may consider that some provision should be made for the older 'missing invoices';

(b) The average invoice value of a purchase invoice may be as little as £40 and with the large volumes being handled, made more difficult by the time delays in receiving invoices and credit notes; a purchase-ledger section can easily become swamped and demoralised by the growing mountain of queries.

**12.28** Returns to publishers can present the following problems:

(a) The returns notes are made out at selling price. The bookseller, therefore, has to reduce the total value of returns to estimated cost for the year-end accounts, and not all publishers allow full credit;

(b) If the bookseller files his copy of the outstanding returns notes in a tray, there will be some doubt as to the completeness of the file of outstanding returns notes, even though each return note is pre-numbered;

(c) Although the bookseller may insist that the prior approval of the publishers has been given before he returned the books (unless the publisher supplied damaged or imperfect books or sent the wrong ones), in many of these instances this approval will have been given over the telephone. Consequently, there is inadequate evidence on the returns note that the return has been authorised and that a credit note will be forthcoming;

(d) Although the bookseller reviews his stock levels regularly, he will probably have a purge in the last few months of his financial year. At the year-end, therefore, the volume of unmatched returns notes may be higher than at any other time during the year. There may be a delay of up to six months before the credit note is received. Consequently, at the time of the annual audit only a small proportion of the returns notes may have been matched with credit notes. The matching process is not helped if the clerk is trying to match returns notes at selling price with credit notes at cost price.

**12.29** The problem over returns is acute with large chains of shops, because of time delays and greater volumes.

**Valuation**

**12.30** As stated above, a bookseller takes stock at selling price. He often holds more than one copy of the same title and if these books were purchased at different times they may show different selling prices. In this case, he values all books at the latest selling price on the basis that this policy does not materially inflate the stock valuation. The auditor may, however, note these older items for follow up with regard to a provision against slow-moving stock.

**12.31** Identifying and recording the selling price of books during a stockcount is relatively straightforward. The difficulty arises in deciding the average buying discount for reducing stock from selling price to cost.

Bearing in mind that selling prices can be determined readily and easily from publishers' invoices, a bookseller with a computerised purchases and/or stock application can input the selling price of each invoice, as well as the purchase price, and produce the average discount by this method. If the purchase invoices are processed manually, the above exercise is not practical. What can be done, however, is to take representative samples of purchase invoices for each category of stock, i.e. paperbacks, retail general hardbacks, retail academic books and school/library supplies. The average buying discounts can be calculated for each sample and these discounts applied to the appropriate categories of stock to reduce the stock valuation from selling price to cost.

The auditor should be involved in the construction of the samples and in agreeing the discounts. He should request that the exercise is repeated every 2–3 years to ensure that the discounts used are up to date.

Stock of postcards, posters and other stationery items will usually be counted at cost price.

The auditor will need to pay special attention to secondhand and antiquarian books, as these are often purchased in job lots and the individual cost prices of items purchased is consequently not available.

**Obsolescence**

**12.32** A significant stock-obsolescence provision should not be necessary at the year-end. An efficient bookseller will have reviewed the stock levels throughout the year and returned slow-moving items to publishers. Books damaged in the shop will have been marked down and sold during the National Book Sale or at some other time during the year.

At the year-end stocktake, any books and stationery items which are damaged or considered to be bad stock, and not returnable to suppliers, should be physically segregated and separately valued at their estimated net-realisable value.

The auditor should question any attempt to raise a general provision of say 1 per cent or 2 per cent against the aggregate amount of good stock. It is unlikely that any good items remaining on the shelves will be marked down to such an extent that they are sold below cost price.

**Accounting policy**

**12.33** A suitable accounting policy on stock to be included in the annual financial statements of a bookshop is as follows:

'Stock is valued at the lower of cost and net-realisable value. Cost is determined by reference to retail selling price less the average buying discount.'

**Tax aspects**

**12.34** Most local inspectors of taxes will reluctantly agree that the only practical method of valuing stock is for it to be counted at selling price and for the resultant valuation to be reduced to estimated cost by reference to the average estimated discount obtained from publishers. If the bookseller and his accountant have difficulties with their inspector, it is likely to be centred on one of the following areas:

(a) confusion over the use of the terms gross margin and discounts from publishers;

(b) evidence that the average discount used is reasonable;

(c) the method by which any stock provision has been calculated.

A long-established bookseller may be using a discount rate agreed many years ago with his local inspector. This rate, however, may no longer bear much relationship to reality, due to the gradual improvement over the years in the terms given by publishers.

**Summary of main problem areas**

**12.35** Computing and auditing the stock valuation of a bookshop is likely to be more straightforward than, for example, most engineering companies and commodity dealers. Particular areas which should be considered during the balance sheet audit of the stock of a bookshop are as follows:

(a) ensuring the completeness and accuracy of the physical stocktake and the build-up of the stock summaries;

(b) checking cut-off, particularly on purchases and returns to publishers;

(c) assessing the reasonability of the discounts used to reduce the stock valuation from selling price to cost;

(d) determining the provision necessary in respect of slow-moving and damaged stock;

(e) valuing stock which has been bought in job/lots, e.g. antiquarian books;

(f) reviewing fluctuations in gross margins and overall stock levels in the absence of analysed trading accounts and the problems listed above.

## Appendix 1

STATEMENT OF STANDARD ACCOUNTING PRACTICE NO. 9

*Stock and Work in Progress*

# 9

# *Stocks and work in progress*

## Contents

# *Stocks and work in progress*

*(Issued May 1975. Part 4 added August 1980)*

*No area of accounting has produced wider differences in practice than the computation of the amount at which stocks and work in progress are stated in financial accounts. This statement of standard accounting practice seeks to define the practices, to narrow the differences and variations in those practices and to ensure adequate disclosure in the accounts.*

## Part 1 – Explanatory note

### Introduction

1 The determination of profit for an accounting year requires the matching of costs with related revenues. The cost of unsold or unconsumed stocks and work in progress will have been incurred in the expectation of future revenue, and when this will not arise until a later year it is appropriate to carry forward this cost to be matched with the revenue when it arises; the applicable concept is the matching of cost and revenue in the year in which the revenue arises rather than in the year in which the cost is incurred. If there is no reasonable expectation of sufficient future revenue to cover cost incurred (e.g., as a result of deterioration, obsolescence or a change in demand), the irrecoverable cost should be charged to revenue in the year under review. Thus, stocks and work in progress normally need to be stated at cost, or, if lower, at net realisable value.

2 The comparison of cost and net realisable value needs to be made in respect of each item of stock separately. Where this is impracticable, groups or categories of stock items which are similar will need to be taken together. To compare the total realisable value of stocks with the total cost could result in an unacceptable setting off of foreseeable losses against unrealised profit.

3 In order to match costs and revenue, 'costs' of stocks and work in progress should comprise that expenditure which has been incurred in the normal course of business in bringing the product or service to its present location and condition. Such costs will include all related production overheads, even though these may accrue on a time basis.

4 The methods used in allocating costs to stocks and work in progress need to be selected with a view to providing the fairest possible approximation to the expenditure actually incurred in bringing the product to its present location and condition. For example, in the case of retail stores holding a large number of rapidly changing individual items, stocks on the shelves have often been stated at current selling prices less the normal gross profit margin. In these particular circumstances this may be acceptable as being the only practical method of arriving at a figure which approximates to cost.

### Net realisable value

5 Net realisable value is the amount at which it is expected that items of stocks and work in progress can be disposed of without creating either profit or loss in the year of sale,

i.e., the estimated proceeds of sale less all further costs to completion and less all costs to be incurred in marketing, selling and distributing directly related to the items in question.

**Replacement cost**

Items of stock and work in progress have sometimes been stated in accounts at estimated replacement cost where this is lower than net realisable value. Where the effect is to take account of a loss greater than that which is expected to be incurred, the use of replacement cost is not regarded as acceptable. However, in some circumstances (e.g., in the case of materials whose price has fluctuated considerably and which have not become the subject of firm sales contracts by the time the accounts are prepared) replacement cost may be the best measure of net realisable value. 6

**Long-term contract work in progress**

Separate consideration needs to be given to work in progress arising from long-term contracts. Owing to the length of time taken to complete such contracts, to defer taking profit into account until completion may result in the profit and loss account reflecting not so much a fair view of the activity of the company during the year but rather the results relating to contracts which have been completed by the year end. It is therefore appropriate to take credit for ascertainable profit while contracts are in progress, subject to the limitations in paragraph 8 below. 7

The profit, if any, taken up needs to reflect the proportion of the work carried out at the accounting date and to take into account any known inequalities of profitability in the various stages of a contract. Many businesses, however, carry out contracts where the outcome cannot reasonably be assessed before the conclusion of the contract and in such cases it is prudent not to take up any profit. Where the business carries out contracts and it is considered that their outcome can be assessed with reasonable certainty before their conclusion, then the attributable profit should be taken up, but the judgement involved should be exercised with prudence. 8

If, however, it is expected that there will be a loss on a contract as a whole, provision needs to be made (in accordance with the prudence concept), for the whole of the loss as soon as it is recognised. This has the effect of reducing the work done to date to its net realisable value. Where unprofitable contracts are of such magnitude that they can be expected to absorb a considerable part of the company's capacity for a substantial period, related administration overheads to be incurred during the period to the completion of those contracts should also be included in the calculation of the provision for losses. 9

Thus, the gross amount of long-term contract work in progress should be stated in accounts at cost plus attributable profits (if any) less foreseeable losses (if any). In arriving at a decision as to whether there are attributable profits, a company should consider whether having regard to the nature of the contracts undertaken it is reasonable to foresee profits in advance of the completion of the contracts. 10

**Disclosure in accounts**

A suitable description of the amount at which stocks and work in progress are stated in accounts might be 'at the lower of cost and net realisable value' or, in the case of long- 11 term contract work in progress, 'at cost plus attributable profit (if any) less foreseeable losses (if any) and progress payments received and receivable'.

12 In order to give an adequate explanation of the affairs of the company the accounting policies followed in arriving at the amount at which stocks and work in progress are stated in the accounts should be set out in a note. Where differing bases have been adopted for different types of stocks and work in progress the amount included in the accounts in respect of each type will need to be stated.

13 In the case of long-term contract work in progress the terms of a contract usually involve progress payments which reduce the amount at which the contract is stated in the accounts. The financial position of a company may be materially dependent on the outcome of such contracts, despite this lessening of their apparent significance. A related note should, therefore, indicate the amount of progress payments received and receivable separately from the net amount of cost plus attributable profit, less foreseeable losses as appropriate.

**Further practical considerations**

14 The basic considerations which must be taken into account in determining costs and net realisable value in relation to stocks and work in progress are set out in Parts 2 and 3 of this statement. The majority of problems which arise in practice in determining both the cost and the net realisable value of stocks and work in progress result from considerations which are relevant to particular businesses and are not of such universal application that they can be the subject of a statement of standard accounting practice. Accordingly, Appendix 1 sets out in more detail some general guidelines which may be of assistance in determining cost and net realisable value and in identifying those situations in which net realisable value is likely to be less than cost. Appendix 1 also sets out considerations which need to be borne in mind in calculating the amount of profit to be taken into account in respect of long-term contracts.

## Part 2 – Definition of terms

15 The following definitions of terms are used for the purpose of this statement.

16 *Stocks and work in progress* comprise:

(a) goods or other assets purchased for resale;

(b) consumable stores;

(c) raw materials and components purchased for incorporation into products for sale;

(d) products and services in intermediate stages of completion;

(e) finished goods.

17 *Cost* is defined in relation to the different categories of stocks and work in progress as being that expenditure which has been incurred in the normal course of business in bringing the product or service to its present location and condition. This expenditure should include, in addition to cost of purchase (as defined in paragraph 18) such costs

of conversion (as defined in paragraph 19) as are appropriate to that location and condition.

*Cost of purchase* comprises purchase price including import duties, transport and handling costs and any other directly attributable costs, less trade discounts, rebates and subsidies. 18

*Cost of conversion* comprises: 19

(a) costs which are specifically attributable to units of production, i.e., direct labour, direct expenses and sub-contracted work;

(b) production overheads (as defined in paragraph 20);

(c) other overheads, if any, attributable in the particular circumstances of the business to bringing the product or service to its present location and condition.

*Production overheads:* overheads incurred in respect of materials, labour or services for production, based on the normal level of activity, taking one year with another. For this purpose each overhead should be classified according to function (e.g., production, selling or administration) so as to ensure the inclusion in cost of conversion of those overheads (including depreciation) which relate to production, notwithstanding that these may accrue wholly or partly on a time basis. 20

*Net realisable value:* the actual or estimated selling price (net of trade but before settlement discounts) less: 21

(a) all further costs to completion; and

(b) all costs to be incurred in marketing, selling and distributing.

*Long-term contract:* a contract entered into for manufacture or building of a single substantial entity or the provision of a service where the time taken to manufacture, build or provide is such that a substantial proportion of all such contract work will extend for a period exceeding one year. 22

*Attributable profit:* that part of the total profit currently estimated to arise over the duration of the contract (after allowing for likely increases in costs so far as not recoverable under the terms of the contract) which fairly reflects the profit attributable to that part of the work performed at the accounting date. (There can be no attributable profit until the outcome of the contract can be assessed with reasonable certainty.) 23

*Foreseeable losses:* losses which are currently estimated to arise over the duration of the contract (after allowing for estimated remedial and maintenance costs, and increases in costs so far as not recoverable under the terms of the contract). This estimate is required irrespective of: 24

(a) whether or not work has yet commenced on such contracts;

(b) the proportion of work carried out at the accounting date;

(c) the amount of profits expected to arise on other contracts.

## Part 3 – Standard accounting practice

25 The expressions used in this statement of standard accounting practice are defined in Part 2.

**Stocks and work in progress other than long-term contract work in progress**

26 The amount at which stocks and work in progress, other than long-term contract work in progress, is stated in periodic financial statements should be the total of the lower of cost and net realisable value of the separate items of stock and work in progress or of groups of similar items.

**Long-term contract work in progress**

27 The amount at which long-term contract work in progress is stated in periodic financial statements should be cost plus any attributable profit, less any foreseeable losses and progress payments received and receivable. If, however, anticipated losses on individual contracts exceed cost incurred to date less progress payments received and receivable, such excesses should be shown separately as provisions.

**Disclosure in financial statements**

28 The accounting policies which have been used in calculating cost, net realisable value, attributable profit and foreseeable losses (as appropriate) should be stated.

29 Stocks and work in progress should be sub-classified in balance sheets or in notes to the financial statements in a manner which is appropriate to the business and so as to indicate the amounts held in each of the main categories.

30 In relation to the amount at which long-term contracts are stated in the balance sheet there should be stated:

(a) the amount of work in progress at cost plus attributable profit, less foreseeable losses;

(b) cash received and receivable at the accounting date as progress payments on account of contracts in progress.

**Date from which effective**

31 The accounting practice set out in this statement should be adopted as soon as possible and regarded as standard in respect of accounts relating to accounting periods starting on or after 1st January 1976.

## Part 4 – Compliance with International Accounting Standards No. 2 'Valuation and presentation of inventories in the context of the historical cost system' and No. 11 'Accounting for construction contracts'

The requirements of International Accounting Standard No. 2 'Valuation and presentation of inventories in the context of the historical cost system' and International Accounting Standard No. 11 'Accounting for construction contracts' accord very closely with the content of the United Kingdom and Irish Accounting Standard No. 9 'Stocks and work in progress' and accordingly compliance with SSAP 9 will ensure compliance with both IAS 2 and IAS 11 in all material aspects.

# Appendix 1

*This appendix is for general guidance and does not form part of the statement of standard accounting practice.*

## FURTHER PRACTICAL CONSIDERATIONS

*Many of the problems involved in arriving at the amount at which stocks and work in progress are stated in accounts are of a practical nature rather than resulting from matters of principle. This appendix discusses some particular areas in which difficulty may be encountered.*

**The allocation of overheads**

Production overheads are included in cost of conversion (as defined in Part 2) together with direct labour, direct expenses and sub-contracted work. This inclusion is a necessary corollary of the principle that expenditure should be included to the extent to which it has been incurred in bringing the product 'to its present location and condition' (paragraph 17 of Part 2). All abnormal conversion costs, however (such as exceptional spoilage, idle capacity and other losses), which are avoidable under normal operating conditions need, for the same reason, to be excluded. 1

Where firm sales contracts have been entered into for the provision of goods or services to customer's specification, overheads relating to design, and marketing and selling costs incurred before manufacture may be included in arriving at cost. 2

The costing methods adopted by a business are usually designed to ensure that all direct material, direct labour, direct expenses and sub-contracted work are identified and charged on a reasonable and consistent basis, but problems arise on the allocation of overheads which must usually involve the exercise of personal judgement in the selection of an appropriate convention. 3

The classification of overheads necessary to achieve this allocation takes the function of the overhead as its distinguishing characteristic (e.g. whether it is a function of production, marketing, selling or administration), rather than whether the overhead tends to vary with time or with volume. 4

The costs of general management, as distinct from functional management, are not directly related to current production and are, therefore, excluded from cost of conversion and hence from the cost of stocks and work in progress. 5

In the case of smaller organisations whose management may be involved in the daily administration of each of the various functions, particular problems may arise in practice in distinguishing these general management overheads. In such organisations the cost of management may fairly be allocated on suitable bases to the functions of production, marketing, selling and administration. 6

Problems may also arise in allocating the costs of central service departments, the allocation of which should depend on the function or functions that the department is serving. For example the accounts department will normally support the following functions: 7

(a) production – by paying production direct and indirect wages and salaries, by controlling purchases and by preparing periodic accounts for the production units;

(b) marketing and distribution – by analysing sales and by controlling the sales ledger;

(c) general administration – by preparing management and annual accounts and budgets, by controlling cash resources and by planning investments.

Only those costs of the accounts department that can reasonably be allocated to the production function fall to be included in the cost of conversion.

8 The allocation of overheads included in the valuation of stocks and work in progress needs to be based on the company's normal level of activity, taking one year with another. The governing factor is that the cost of unused capacity should be written off in the current year. In determining what constitutes 'normal' the following factors need to be considered:

(a) the volume of production which the production facilities are intended by their designers and by management to produce under the working conditions (e.g. single or double shift) prevailing during the year;

(b) the budgeted level of activity for the year under review and for the ensuing year;

(c) the level of activity achieved both in the year under review and in previous years.

Although temporary changes in the load of activity may be ignored, persistent variation should lead to a revision of the previous norm.

9 Where management accounts are prepared on a marginal cost basis, it will be necessary to add to the figure of stock so arrived at the appropriate proportion of those production overheads not already included in the marginal cost.

10 The adoption of a conservative approach to the valuation of stocks and work in progress has sometimes been used as one of the reasons for omitting selected production overheads. In so far as the circumstances of the business require an element of prudence in determining the amount at which stocks and work in progress are stated, this needs to be taken into account in the determination of net realisable value and not by the exclusion from cost of selected overheads.

**Methods of costing**

11 It is frequently not practicable to relate expenditure to specific units of stocks and work in progress. The ascertainment of the nearest approximation to cost gives rise to two problems:

(a) the selection of an appropriate method for relating costs to stocks and work in progress (e.g. job costing, batch costing, process costing, standard costing);

(b) the selection of an appropriate method for calculating the related cost where a number of identical items have been purchased or made at different times (e.g. unit cost, average cost or FIFO).

In selecting the methods referred to in paragraphs 11 (a) and (b) above, management must exercise judgement to ensure that the methods chosen provide the fairest practicable approximation to 'actual cost'. Furthermore, where standard costs are used they need to be reviewed frequently to ensure that they bear a reasonable relationship to actual costs obtaining during the period. Methods such as base stock and LIFO do not usually bear such a relationship. 12

The method of arriving at cost by applying the latest purchase price to the total number of units in stock is unacceptable in principle because it is not necessarily the same as actual cost and, in times of rising prices, will result in the taking of a profit which has not been realised. 13

One method of arriving at cost, in the absence of a satisfactory costing system, is the use of selling price less an estimated profit margin. This is acceptable only if it can be demonstrated that the method gives a reasonable approximation of the actual cost. 14

In industries where the cost of minor by-products is not separable from the cost of the principal products, stocks of such by-products may be stated in accounts at their net realisable value. In this case the costs of the main products are calculated after deducting the net realisable value of the by-products. 15

**The determination of net realisable value**

The initial calculation of provisions to reduce stocks from cost to net realisable value may often be made by the use of formulae based on predetermined criteria. The formulae normally take account of the age, movements during the past, expected future movements and estimated scrap values of the stock, as appropriate. Whilst the use of such formulae establishes a basis for making a provision which can be consistently applied, it is still necessary for the results to be reviewed in the light of any special circumstances which cannot be anticipated in the formulae, such as changes in the state of the order book. 16

Where a provision is required to reduce the value of finished goods below cost, the stocks of the parts and sub-assemblies held for the purpose of the manufacture of such products, together with stocks on order, need to be reviewed to determine if provision is also required against such items. 17

Where stocks of spares are held for sale special consideration of the factors in paragraph 16 of this appendix will be required in the context of: 18

(a) the number of units sold to which they are applicable;

(b) the estimated frequency with which a replacement spare is required;

(c) the expected useful life of the unit to which they are applicable.

Events occurring between the balance sheet date and the date of completion of the accounts need to be considered in arriving at the net realisable value at the balance sheet date (e.g. a subsequent reduction in selling prices). However, no reduction falls to be made when the realisable value of material stocks is less than the purchase price provided that the goods into which the materials are to be incorporated can still be sold at a profit after incorporating the materials at cost price. 19

**The application of net realisable value**

20 The principal situations in which net realisable value is likely to be less than cost are where there has been:

(a) an increase in costs or a fall in selling price;

(b) physical deterioration of stocks;

(c) obsolescence of products;

(d) a decision as part of a company's marketing strategy to manufacture and sell products at a loss;

(e) errors in production or purchasing.

Furthermore, when stocks are held which are unlikely to be sold within the turnover period normal in that company (i.e. excess stocks), the impending delay in realisation increases the risk that the situations outlined in (a) to (c) above may occur before the stocks are sold and needs to be taken into account in assessing net realisable value.

**Long-term contract work in progress**

21 In ascertaining cost of long-term contract work in progress it is not normally appropriate to include interest payable on borrowed money. However, in those infrequent circumstances where sums borrowed can be identified as financing specific long-term contracts, it may be appropriate to include such related interest in cost, in which circumstances the facts should be clearly stated.

22 In some businesses, long-term contracts for the supply of services or manufacture and supply of goods exist where the prices are determined and invoiced according to separate parts of the contract. In these businesses the most appropriate method of reflecting profits on each contract is usually to match costs against performance of the separable parts of the contract, treating each such separable part as a separate contract. In such instances, however, future revenues from the contract need to be compared with future estimated costs and provision made for any foreseen loss.

23 In determining whether there is attributable profit to be included in the amount at which long-term contract work in progress is stated in the accounts, and in calculating such attributable profit, account should be taken of the type of business concerned. It is necessary to define the earliest point for each particular contract before which no profit is taken up, the overriding principle being that there can be no attributable profit until the outcome of a contract can reasonably be foreseen. Of the profit which in the light of all the circumstances can be foreseen with a reasonable degree of certainty to arise on completion of the contract, there should be regarded as earned to date only that part which prudently reflects the amount of work performed to date. The method used for taking up such profits needs to be consistently applied.

24 In calculating the total estimated profit on the contract, it is necessary to take into account not only the total costs to date and the total estimated further costs to completion (calculated by reference to the same principles as were applied to cost to date) but also the estimated future costs of rectification and guarantee work, and any other future work to be undertaken under the terms of the contract. These are then compared with the total sales value of the contract. In considering future costs it is necessary to

have regard to likely increases in wages and salaries, to likely increases in the price of raw materials and to rises in general overheads so far as these items are not recoverable from the customer under the terms of the contract.

Where approved variations have been made to a contract in the course of it and the amount to be received in respect of these variations has not yet been settled and is likely to be a material factor in the outcome, it is necessary to make a conservative estimate of the amount likely to be received and this is then treated as part of the total sales value. On the other hand, provision needs to be made for foreseen claims or penalties payable arising out of delays in completion or from other causes. 25

The settlement of claims arising from circumstances not envisaged in the contract or arising as an indirect consequence of approved variations is subject to a high level of uncertainty relating to the outcome of future negotiations. In view of this, it is generally prudent to make provision for receipts in respect of such claims only when negotiations have reached an advanced stage and there is evidence in writing of the acceptability of the claim in principle to the purchaser, an indication of the magnitude of the sum involved also being available. 26

The amount to be reflected in the year's profit and loss account will be the appropriate proportion of this total profit by reference to the work done to date, less any profit already taken up in prior years. The estimated outcome of a contract which extends over several accounting years will nearly always vary in the light of changes in circumstances and for this reason the result of the year will not necessarily represent the proportion of the total profit on the contract which is appropriate to the amount of work carried out in the period: it may also reflect the effect of changes in circumstances during the year which affect the total profit estimated to accrue on completion. 27

## Appendix 2

*This appendix is for general guidance and does not form part of the statement of standard accounting practice.*

### GLOSSARY OF TERMS

*The use of the following terms in describing the accounting policies adopted in arriving at the amount at which stocks and work in progress are stated in accounts should be restricted in conformity with the definitions given to each. Where these definitions are inapplicable, alternative expressions should be used and explained.*

*Unit cost:* the cost of purchasing or manufacturing identifiable units of stock. 1

*Average cost:* the calculation of the cost of stocks and work in progress on the bases of the application to the unit of stocks on hand of an average price computed by dividing the total cost of units by the total number of such units. This average price may be arrived at by means of a continuous calculation, a periodic calculation or a moving periodic calculation. 2

3 *FIFO (first in, first out):* the calculation of the cost of stocks and work in progress on the basis that the quantities in hand represent the latest purchases or production.

4 *LIFO (last in, first out):* the calculation of the cost of stocks and work in progress on the basis that the quantities in hand represent the earliest purchases or production.

5 *Base stock:* the calculation of the cost of stocks and work in progress on the basis that a fixed unit value is ascribed to a predetermined number of units of stock, any excess over this number being valued on the basis of some other method. If the number of units in stock is less than the predetermined minimum, the fixed unit value is applied to the number in stock.

6 *Replacement cost:* the cost at which an identical asset could be purchased or manufactured.

7 *Standard cost:* the calculation of the cost of stocks and work in progress on the basis of periodically predetermined costs calculated from management's estimates of expected levels of costs and of operations and operational efficiency and the related expenditure.

8 *Completed long-term contract:* a long-term contract on which no further work, apart from maintenance work, is expected to take place.

## Appendix 3

*This appendix is for general guidance and does not form part of the statement of standard accounting practice.*

STOCK-IN-TRADE AND WORK IN PROGRESS

**Inland Revenue practice with regard to a change in the basis of stock valuation on the adoption of SSAP 9 (Statement 2.109).**

References in this statement to 'N22' relate to a Council recommendation *Treatment of stock-in-trade and work in progress in financial statements* which was withdrawn from the *Members' Handbook* on the introduction of SSAP 9.

At meetings on 7th May 1975 and 2nd August 1978 the Council authorised the publication of the following statement and supplementary statement, respectively:

## Statement of 7th May 1975

**Changes in basis of valuation**

1. After the publication of **N22**, the Revenue explained their practice with regard to changes in the basis of valuation in a statement published in *The Accountant* on 17th

November 1962. The practice set out in that statement applies to changes made as a result of the adoption of SSAP 9 in the following way. References to stock-in-trade cover manufacturing work in progress but not professional work in progress or work under long-term contracts.

2. First, the basis set out in SSAP 9 will be regarded as a valid basis, and will be accepted as a good reason for a change from a previously valid basis. Therefore on such a change the opening stock of the year of change is to be valued on the same basis as the closing stock of that year. Whether the change is to a higher or lower level, the valuations of previous years will not be revised. Further assessments for past years will not therefore be raised nor will relief under the 'error or mistake' provisions be admitted on this account.

3. Where the existing basis of stock valuation is valid under recommendation **N22** and is such that the adoption of the new standard could be argued to be merely a refinement and not a change of basis, the Revenue will be prepared to accept a valuation of the opening stock in the year of change by reference to the new standard, i.e., the argument that there has only been a refinement, so that the opening valuation should be the same as the closing valuation of the preceding year, will not be used.

4. Where stock has been brought into accounts in the past on a basis which was not a valid basis under recommendation **N22**, the Revenue must reserve the right to review past liabilities. However, where there is no question of past irregularities (i.e. fraud, wilful default or neglect), the Revenue would not in any event seek to recover tax for past years on an amount greater than that involved in the uplift of the closed valuation of the year preceding the year of change to a valid basis within the old code.

5. These comments are made on the basis of existing law and practice. The Revenue reserve the right to reconsider their attitude in the event of any change in the law, and in any case, at the expiry of 3 years.

**Discounted selling price**

6. Where stock is valued at current selling prices less the normal gross profit margin in the circumstances described in paragraph 4 of Part 1 of the statement, the valuation will be acceptable only if the further test set out in paragraph 14 of Appendix 1 to the statement is clearly satisfied.

It is considered that the selling price to be used for the purpose of discounting should normally be the original price fixed for the article determined by operating the normal mark-up on the original cost price.

**Replacement cost**

7. Where the value of the raw material content forms a high proportion of the total value of stock in process of production and the price of the raw materials is liable to considerable fluctuation, it is common practice to make rapid changes in selling prices to accord with the changes in the price of the raw material. In cases of this kind the replacement cost basis may be extended to cover stock in process of production and finished stock as well as to the stocks of raw material.

**Long-term contracts**

8. Where a loss on a contract as a whole is foreseen, a proportion of the overall loss, calculated either by reference to time normally up to the due completion date under the terms of the contract, or to expenditure incurred, may normally be taken into account year by year during the remainder of the contract period so long as all contracts, profitable or otherwise, are dealt with similarly. Further, when the work on a long-term contract has been substantially completed, so that it is possible to assess the financial outcome of the contract with reasonable certainty, the Inland Revenue do not normally object to account being taken, at that point, of the foreseeable further expenditure representing obligations arising out of the contract up to the time of final delivery and also of a reasonable provision to allow for expenditure under any guarantee or warranties included in the contract. Beyond these limits it is not permissible for tax purposes to take account of expenditure which has not then been incurred. It follows that a provision for an expected future loss made in accordance with paragraph 9 of Part 1 of the statement would be disallowed for tax purposes to the extent that it is in excess of the amount determined above.

9. Where there is a change in the basis for treatment of long-term contracts, the opening figure in the year of change must, for taxation purposes, be the same as the closing figure for the preceding year.

The Inland Revenue will not accept a claim for a tax-free uplift based on the grounds that the opening and closing figures in the year of change must be on the same basis. Alternatively, the Inland Revenue would accept the continuance of the existing basis for long-term contracts current at the beginning of the year of change, with the new basis being applied only to contracts entered into in or after the year of change.

## Supplementary Statement of 2nd August 1978

10. The Inland Revenue confirm that even if the taxpayer has prepared his accounts for the year of change on a basis that values all long-term contracts in accordance with SSAP9, he may nevertheless make an adjustment in his tax computation for that year to give effect to the concluding sentence of paragraph (9) above. Therefore any uplift on an existing valuation made solely to conform to SSAP9 either at the commencement of the year of change or during that year in respect of contracts in existence at the commencement of that year will be ignored for tax purposes. The profit on those contracts will be brought into charge for tax purposes on whatever basis the taxpayer has hitherto adopted, and this will therefore mean similar adjustments in subsequent years until those contracts are run off.

11. A change in the basis of valuation of stock or work in progress will normally lead to a revision of stock relief (Finance Act 1976, Schedule 5, paragraph 24). However, the Inland Revenue also confirm that they will not seek to apply paragraph 24 where a taxpayer changes his basis of valuation of long-term contracts in order to comply with SSAP9, but, at least so far as his tax computation is concerned, does so in accordance with paragraph (10) above. There will, therefore, be no restriction of stock relief in those circumstances.

12. Therefore in these circumstances old contracts would be run off as explained in paragraph (10) above, and there will be no restriction of stock relief in the case of new contracts.

13. The Inland Revenue confirm that the above comments apply to the accounting period in which a change is made to comply with SSAP9 (and to any subsequent accounting period in which old contracts are still being run off), provided that the accounting period commences on or after 1st January 1976 (when SSAP9 became standard practice). This, however, is subject to compliance with the existing time limits for claiming stock relief.

## Appendix 2

STATEMENT OF INTERNATIONAL ACCOUNTING PRACTICE NO. 2

*Valuation and Presentation of Inventories in the Context of the Historical Cost System*

# Preface to International Accounting Standard No. 2 "Valuation and Presentation of Inventories in the Context of the Historical Cost System"

**This Preface has been approved by the Councils of the following accountancy bodies for publication to their respective members:**

**The Institute of Chartered Accountants in England and Wales**
**The Institute of Chartered Accountants of Scotland**
**The Institute of Chartered Accountants in Ireland**
**The Association of Certified Accountants**
**The Institute of Cost and Management Accountants**
**The Chartered Institute of Public Finance and Accountancy**

The status of International Accounting Standards is set out in the "Introduction to International Accounting Standards". The International Accounting Standard which follows is for application to the published annual accounts of commercial, industrial and business enterprises in the UK or Ireland and of overseas subsidiaries and associated companies where these accounts are to be incorporated in group accounts in the UK or Ireland. Members should note that this International Accounting Standard accords closely with the content of the UK and Irish Accounting Standard No. 9 "Stocks and Work in Progress". Compliance with that standard will ensure compliance with this International Accounting Standard.

# Contents

# Introduction

1. This Statement deals with the valuation and presentation of inventories[1] in financial statements in the context of the historical cost system, which is the most widely adopted basis on which financial statements are presented.

2. The Committee is aware of other systems that are proposed or used in financial statements, including systems that are based on replacement costs or other current values. Inventory valuation and presentation in the context of those other systems are beyond the scope of this Statement. International Accounting Standard 1, *Disclosure of Accounting Policies,* requires that the system adopted must be clearly stated.

3. This Statement does not deal with inventories accumulated under long-term construction contracts and with inventory treatment of by-products.

## Definitions

4. The following terms are used in this Statement with the meanings specified.

*Inventories* are tangible property (a) held for sale in the ordinary course of business, (b) in the process of production for such sale, or (c) to be consumed in the production of goods or services for sale.

*Historical cost* of inventories is the aggregate of costs of purchase, costs of conversion, and other costs incurred in bringing the inventories to their present location and condition.

*Costs of purchase* comprise the purchase price including import duties and other purchase taxes, transport and handling costs, and any other directly attributable costs of acquisition less trade discounts, rebates, and subsidies.

*Costs of conversion* are those costs, in addition to the costs of purchase, that relate to bringing the inventories to their present location and condition.

[1]The term "inventories" is used throughout this Statement; in some countries inventories are described as "stock and work in progress."

*Net realisable value* is the estimated selling price in the ordinary course of business less costs of completion and less costs necessarily to be incurred in order to make the sale.

# Explanation

5. Inventories comprise a significant portion of the assets of many enterprises. The valuation and presentation of inventories therefore have a significant effect in determining and presenting the financial position and results of operations of those enterprises.

## Determination of Historical Cost

6. In determining historical cost as defined in paragraph 4, different interpretations arise in practice as regards production overhead, other overheads, and the cost formula to be used.

### Production Overhead

7. Production overhead is comprised of costs incurred for production other than direct materials and labour. Examples are indirect materials and labour, depreciation and maintenance of factory buildings and equipment, and the cost of factory management and administration.

8. Production overhead requires analysis to determine the portion related to bringing the inventories to their present location and condition and thus to be included in the costs of conversion when determining the historical cost of inventories.

9. Both fixed and variable production overhead incurred during production are usually allocated to costs of conversion. That practice is based on the view that they are both incurred in putting inventories in their present location and condition. Fixed production overhead is sometimes excluded in whole or in part from costs of conversion on the grounds that it is not considered to relate directly to putting inventories in their present location and condition.

10. In a period of low production or if there is idle plant, it is customary to restrict the allocation of fixed production overhead to the costs of conversion by relating it to the capacity of the production facilities and not to the actual level of throughput. Capacity of the production facilities is variously interpreted, for example, as the normal production expected to be achieved over a number of periods or seasons or as the maximum production that as a practical matter can be achieved. The interpretation is determined in advance and applied consistently, and is not modified for temporary conditions.

11. Similarly, exceptional amounts of waste—material, labour, or other expenses—which do not relate to bringing the inventories to their present location and condition are excluded from conversion costs.

## Other Overheads

12. Overheads other than production overhead are sometimes incurred in bringing inventories to their present location and condition, for example, expenditures incurred in designing products for specific customers. On the other hand, selling expenses, general administrative overheads, research and development costs, and interest are usually considered not to relate to putting the inventories in their present location and condition.

## Cost Formula Used

13. Several different formulas with widely different effects are in current use for the purpose of assigning costs, including the following:

(a) First-in, first-out (FIFO)

(b) Weighted average cost

(c) Last-in, first-out (LIFO)

(d) Base stock

(e) Specific identification

(f) Next-in, first-out (NIFO)

(g) Latest purchase price.

14. The FIFO, weighted average cost, LIFO, base stock, and specific identification formulas use costs that have been incurred by the enterprise at one time or another. The NIFO and latest purchase price methods use costs that have not all been incurred and are therefore not based on historical cost.

15. Specific identification is a formula that attributes specific costs to identified items of inventory. This is an appropriate treatment for goods that have been bought or manufactured and are segregated for a specific project. If it is used, however, in respect of items of inventory which are ordinarily interchangeable, the selection of items could be made in such a way as to obtain predetermined effects on profit.

## Valuation of Inventories Below Historical Cost

16. The historical cost of inventories may not be realisable if their selling prices have declined, if they are damaged, or if they have become wholly or partially obsolete. The practice of writing inventories down below historical cost to net realisable value accords with the view that current assets should not be carried in excess of amounts expected to be realised. Declines in value are computed separately for individual items, groups of similar items, an entire class of inventory (for example, finished goods), or items relating to a class of business, or they are computed on an overall basis for all the inventories of the enterprise. The practice of writing inventories down based on a class of inventory, on a class of business, or on an overall basis results in offsetting losses incurred against unrealised gains.

17. In some countries, writedowns are made which are not based on the practices described in paragraph 16. For example, writedowns below historical cost are arrived at by applying an arbitrary percentage to the amounts otherwise computed or by undisclosed reductions that result in secret reserves; these produce inappropriate effects on financial statements.

## Presentation of Inventories

18. The sub-classification of inventories in financial statements informs readers of the amounts held in different categories and the extent of the changes from period to period. Common sub-classifications are materials, work in progress, finished goods, merchandise, and production supplies.

19. "Inventories" in balance sheets usually consist of items included in the definition of inventories in paragraph 4. Other items are sometimes shown under the heading "Inventories", for example, non-production supplies and research and development supplies.

# International Accounting Standard 2
## Valuation and Presentation of Inventories in the Context of the Historical Cost System

*International Accounting Standard 2 comprises paragraphs 20—36 of this Statement. The Standard should be read in the context of paragraphs 1—19 of this Statement and of the Preface to Statements of International Accounting Standards.*

**20. Inventories should be valued at the lower of historical cost and net realisable value.**

### Ascertainment of Historical Cost

**21. The historical cost of manufactured inventories should include a systematic allocation of those production overhead costs that relate to putting the inventories in their present location and condition. Allocation of fixed production overhead to the costs of conversion should be based on the capacity of the facilities. If fixed production overhead has been entirely or substantially excluded from the valuation of inventories on the grounds that it does not directly relate to putting the inventories in their present location and condition, that fact should be disclosed.**

**22. Overheads other than production overhead should be included as part of inventory cost only to the extent that they clearly relate to putting the inventories in their present location and condition.**

**23. Exceptional amounts of wasted material, labour, or other expenses should not be included as part of inventory cost.**

**24. Except as set out in paragraphs 25 and 26, the historical cost of inventories should be accounted for using the FIFO formula or a weighted average cost formula.**

**25. Inventories of items that are not ordinarily interchangeable or goods manufactured and segregated for specific projects should be accounted for by using specific identification of their individual costs.**

**26. The LIFO or base stock formulas may be used provided that there is disclosure of the difference between the amount of the inventories as shown in the balance sheet and either (a) the lower of the amount arrived at in accordance with paragraph 24 and net realisable value or (b) the lower of current cost at the balance sheet date and net realisable value.**

**27. Techniques such as the standard cost method of valuing products or the retail method of valuing merchandise may be used for convenience if they approximate consistently the results that would be obtained in accordance with paragraph 20.**

## Ascertainment of Net Realisable Value

**28. Estimates of net realisable value should be based not on temporary fluctuations of price or cost but on the most reliable evidence available at the time the estimates are made as to what the inventories are expected to realise.**

**29. Inventories should be written down to net realisable value item by item or by groups of similar items; whichever method is used should be consistently applied.**

**30. The net realisable value of the quantity of inventory held to satisfy firm sales contracts should be based on the contract price. If the sales contracts are for less than the inventory quantities held, net realisable value for the excess should be based on general market prices.[2]**

**31. Normal quantities of materials and other supplies held for incorporation in the production of goods should not be written down below historical cost if the finished products in which they will be incorporated are expected to be realised at or above historical cost. Nevertheless, a decline in the price of materials may indicate that the historical cost of finished products to be produced will exceed net realisable value in which event a writedown of the materials inventories should be made; in this event, replacement cost may be the best available measure of the net realisable value of those materials.**

[2] Firm sales contracts beyond inventory quantities held, and firm purchase contracts are beyond the scope of this Statement.

## Presentation in the Financial Statements

**32. The profit and loss of the period should be charged with the amount of inventories sold or used (unless allocated to other asset accounts) and with the amount of any writedown in the period to net realisable value.**

**33. Inventories should be sub-classified in balance sheets or in notes to the financial statements in a manner which is appropriate to the business and so as to indicate the amounts held in each of the main categories.**

**34. The accounting policies adopted for the purpose of valuation of inventories, including the cost formula used, should be disclosed. A change in an accounting policy related to inventories that has a material effect in the current period or may have a material effect in subsequent periods should be disclosed together with the reasons. The effect of the change should, if material, be disclosed and quantified. (See International Accounting Standard 1, Disclosure of Accounting Policies.)**

**35. If items are shown under the caption "Inventories" other than those comprehended by the definition in paragraph 4, their nature, amounts and basis of valuation should be disclosed.**

## Effective Date

**36. This International Accounting Standard becomes operative for financial statements covering periods beginning on or after 1 January 1976.**

## Appendix 3

STATEMENT OF INTERNATIONAL ACCOUNTING PRACTICE NO. 11

*Accounting for Construction Costs*

# APPLICATION IN THE UK AND IRELAND OF INTERNATIONAL ACCOUNTING STANDARD NO. 11

## Accounting for Construction Contracts

This International Accounting Standard was published by the IASC in March 1979. It is published in the UK and Ireland by the Councils of the six accountancy bodies forming the CCAB*, for the information of persons interested in financial reporting.

The six Councils of the accountancy bodies comprising the CCAB support the activities of the IASC in promoting world-wide harmonisation of accounting standards and support the standards issued by the IASC. The Councils implement their support of international standards by seeking to incorporate the provisions of IASs within the body of UK and Irish SSAPs in so far as the provisions are not included in the law.

International accounting standards (to the extent they are not already covered by legal requirements or national standards) come into effect when their provisions are incorporated into SSAPs issued by the Councils of the UK and Irish bodies: they do not override UK and Irish law and SSAPs.

Compliance with company law and SSAPs in the UK and Ireland will automatically ensure conformity with International Accounting Standard No. 11 *Accounting for Construction Contracts.*

---

* The Institute of Chartered Accountants in England and Wales
The Institute of Chartered Accountants of Scotland
The Institute of Chartered Accountants in Ireland
The Association of Certified Accountants
The Institute of Cost and Management Accountants
The Chartered Institute of Public Finance and Accountancy

# Contents

# Introduction

1. This Statement deals with accounting for construction contracts in the financial statements of contractors.

2. For the purposes of this Statement a construction contract is a contract for the construction of an asset or of a combination of assets which together constitute a single project. Examples of activity covered by such contracts include the construction of bridges, dams, ships, buildings and complex pieces of equipment.

3. The feature which characterises a construction contract dealt with in this Statement is the fact that the date at which the contract activity is entered into and the date when the contract activity is completed fall into different accounting periods. The specific duration of the contract performance is not used as a distinguishing feature of a construction contract.

4. Contracts for the provision of services come within the scope of this Statement to the extent that they are directly related to a contract for the construction of an asset. Examples of such service contracts are contracts for the services of project managers and architects and for technical engineering services related to the construction of an asset.

# Explanation

5. The principal problem relating to accounting for construction contracts is the allocation of revenues and related costs to accounting periods over the duration of the contract.

## Types of Construction Contracts

6. Construction contracts are formulated in a variety of ways, but generally fall into two basic types:

(a) fixed price contracts—the contractor agrees to a fixed contract price, or rate, in some cases subject to cost escalation clauses

(b) cost plus contracts—the contractor is reimbursed for allowable or otherwise defined costs, plus a percentage of these costs or a fixed fee.

Both types of contract are within the scope of this Statement.

## The Accounting Treatment of Construction Contract Costs and Revenues

7. Two methods of accounting for contracts commonly followed by contractors are the 'percentage of completion' method and the 'completed contract' method.

8. Under the percentage of completion method, revenue is recognised as the contract activity progresses. The costs incurred in reaching the stage of completion are matched with this revenue, resulting in the reporting of results which can be attributed to the proportion of work completed.

9. Under the completed contract method, revenue is recognised only when the contract is completed or substantially completed; that is, when only minor work is expected other than warranty work. Costs and progress payments received are accumulated during the course of the contract but revenue is not recognised until the contract activity is substantially completed.

10. Under both methods, provision is made for losses for the stage of completion reached on the contract. In addition, provision is usually made for losses on the remainder of the contract.

11. It may be necessary for accounting purposes to combine contracts made with a single customer or to combine contracts made with several customers if the contracts are negotiated as a package or if the contracts are for a single project. Conversely, if a contract covers a number of projects and if the costs and revenues of such individual projects can be identified within the terms of the overall contract, each such project may be treated as equivalent to a separate contract.

## The Costs to be Accumulated for Construction Contracts

12. The total period to be considered for identifying the costs attributable to a contract is the period that commences with the securing of the contract and closes when the contract is completed.

13. Therefore, costs incurred by the contractor before a contract is secured are usually treated as expenses of the period in which they are incurred. However, if costs attributable to securing the contract can be separately identified and there is a clear indication that the contract will be obtained, the costs are often treated as applicable to the contract and are deferred. As a practical matter, costs are sometimes deferred until it is clear whether the contract has been secured or not.

14. Costs attributable to a contract include expected warranty costs. Warranty costs are provided for when such costs can be reasonably estimated (see International Accounting Standard 10, Contingencies and Events Occurring After the Balance Sheet Date).

15. The costs incurred by an enterprise that undertakes construction contracts can be divided into:

(a) Costs that relate directly to a specific contract
(b) Costs that can be attributed to the contract activity in general and can be allocated to specific contracts
(c) Costs that relate to the activities of the enterprise generally, or that relate to contract activity but cannot be related to specific contracts.

16. Examples of costs that relate directly to a specific contract include:

site labour costs, including supervision;
materials used for project construction;
depreciation of plant and equipment used on a contract;
costs of moving plant and equipment to and from a site.

17. Examples of costs that can be attributed to the contract activity in general and can be allocated to specific contracts include:

insurance;
design and technical assistance;
construction overhead.

18. Examples of costs that relate to the activities of the enterprise generally, or that relate to contract activity but cannot be related to specific contracts, include:

general administration and selling costs;
finance costs;
research and development costs;
depreciation of idle plant and equipment that is not used on a particular contract.

19. Costs referred to in paragraph 18 are usually excluded from the accumulated contract costs because they do not relate to reaching the present stage of completion of a specific contract. However, in some circumstances general administrative expenses, development costs and finance costs are specifically attributable to a particular contract and are sometimes included as part of accumulated contract costs.

## The Basis for Recognising Revenue on Construction Contracts

### The Percentage of Completion Method

20. Under the percentage of completion method, the amount of revenue recognised is determined by reference to the stage of completion of the contract activity at the end of each accounting period. The advantage of this method of accounting for contract revenue is that it reflects revenue in the accounting period during which activity was undertaken to earn such revenue.

21. The stage of completion used to determine revenue to be recognised in the financial statements can be measured in a variety of ways; for example, by calculating the proportion that costs incurred to date bear to the estimated total costs of the contract, by surveys which measure work performed and completion of a physical proportion of the contract work or by a combination of ways.

22. Progress payments and advances received from customers do not necessarily reflect the stage of completion and therefore cannot usually be treated as equivalent to revenue earned.

23. If the percentage of completion method is applied by calculating the proportion that costs to date bear to the latest estimated total costs of the contract, adjustments are made to include only those costs that reflect work performed. Examples of items which may need adjustment include:

(a) the costs of materials that have been purchased for the contract but have not been installed or used during contract performance, and

(b) payments to subcontractors to the extent that they do not reflect the amount of work performed under the sub-contract.

24. The application of the percentage of completion method is subject to a risk of error in making estimates. For this reason, profit is not recognised in the financial statements unless the outcome of the contract can be reliably estimated. If the outcome can not be reliably estimated, the percentage of completion method is not used.

25. In the case of fixed price contracts, the conditions which will usually provide this degree of reliability are:

(a) total contract revenues to be received can be reliably estimated, and

(b) both the costs to complete the contract and the stage of contract performance completed at the reporting date can be reliably estimated, and

(c) the costs attributable to the contract can be clearly identified so that actual experience can be compared with prior estimates.

26. In the case of cost plus contracts, the conditions which will usually provide this degree of reliability are:

(a) the costs attributable to the contract can be clearly identified, and

(b) costs other than those that will be specifically reimbursable under the contract can be reliably estimated.

## The Completed Contract Method

27. The principal advantage of the completed contract method is that it is based on results as determined when the contract is completed or substantially completed rather than on estimates which may require subsequent adjustment as a result of unforeseen costs and possible losses. The risk of recognising profits that may not have been earned is therefore minimised.

28. The principal disadvantage of the completed contract method is that periodic reported income does not reflect the level of activity on contracts during the period. For example, when a few large contracts are completed in one accounting period but no contracts have been completed in the previous period or will be completed in the subsequent period, the level of reported income can be erratic although the level of activity on contracts may have been relatively constant throughout. Even when numerous contracts are regularly completed in each accounting period, and reported income may appear to reflect the level of activity

on contracts, there is a continuous lag between the time when work is performed and the related revenue is recognised.

## Selection of Method

29. The selection of a method of accounting for a construction contract depends on the view taken by the contractor in respect of the uncertainties attached to the estimates of contract costs and revenues. In some cases, the contractor may decide that the level of uncertainty, produced by variations in work which render recoverable costs and revenue subject to further negotiation or by the inherent problem of making estimates, is so significant that the completed contract method is applied. In other cases, the outcome of the contracts can be reliably estimated and some or all of the contracts may be accounted for using the percentage of completion method. The contractor may be using both methods simultaneously for different contracts.

30. When a contractor uses a method for a particular contract, then all other contracts that meet similar criteria ought to be accounted for by the same method.

31. In addition to the consideration of uncertainties, a contractor may use pre-determined criteria for the selection of an accounting method for construction contracts. For example, contracts for which the revenue is less than a stated value, or which have a duration of less than a certain period of time, may be accounted for by the completed contract method even when the outcome of contracts can be reliably estimated.

32. The methods of accounting used by the contractor and the criteria adopted in selecting the methods represent an accounting policy that is consistently applied (see International Accounting Standard 1, Disclosure of Accounting Policies).

## Change in Accounting Policy

33. When there is a change in the accounting policy used for construction contracts, there is disclosure of the effect of the change and its amount, together with the reasons for the change (see International Accounting Standard 8, Unusual and Prior Period Items and Changes in Accounting Policies). If the contractor changes from the percentage of completion

method to the completed contract method, it may not be possible to quantify the full effect of the change in the current accounting period. In such cases, there is disclosure in respect of contracts in progress at the beginning of the accounting period of at least the amount of attributable profits reported in prior years.

## Provision for Foreseeable Losses

34. When current estimates of total contract costs and revenues indicate a loss, provision is made for the entire loss on the contract irrespective of the amount of work done. In some circumstances, the foreseeable losses may exceed the costs of work done to date. Provision is nevertheless made for the entire loss on the contract.

35. When a contract is of such magnitude that it can be expected to absorb a considerable part of the capacity of the enterprise for a substantial period, indirect costs to be incurred during the period of the completion of the contract are sometimes considered to be directly attributable to the contract and included in the calculation of the provision for loss on the contract.

36. If a provision for loss is required, the amount of such provision is usually determined irrespective of:

(a) whether or not work has commenced on the contract, and
(b) the stage of completion of contract activity, and
(c) the amount of profits expected to arise on other unrelated contracts.

37. The determination of a future loss on a contract may be subject to a high degree of uncertainty. In some cases, it may be possible to accrue the future loss and in other cases only the existence of a contingent loss is disclosed (see International Accounting Standard 10, Contingencies and Events Occurring After the Balance Sheet Date).

## Claims and Variations Arising Under Construction Contracts

38. Amounts due in respect of claims made by the contractor and of variations in contract work approved by the customer are recognised as revenue in the financial statements only in circumstances when, and only to the extent that, the contractor has evidence of the acceptability of the amount of the claim or variation.

39. Claims or penalties payable by the contractor arising out of delays in completion or from other causes are provided for in full in the financial statements as costs attributable to the contract. Claims in the nature of contingencies are treated in accordance with International Accounting Standard 10, Contingencies and Events Occurring After the Balance Sheet Date.

## Progress Payments, Advances and Retentions

40. Progress payments and advances received from customers in respect of construction contracts are disclosed in financial statements either shown as a deduction from the amount of contract work in progress or as a liability.

41. Progress payments due but not received and amounts retained by customers until the satisfaction of conditions specified in the contract for release of such amounts are either recognised in financial statements as receivables or alternatively indicated by way of a note.

# International Accounting Standard 11

# Accounting for Construction Contracts

*International Accounting Standard 11 comprises paragraphs 42-49 of this Statement. The Standard should be read in the context of paragraphs 1-41 of this Statement and of the Preface to Statements of International Accounting Standards.*

**42. In accounting for construction contracts in financial statements, either the percentage of completion method or the completed contract method should be used.**

**43. The percentage of completion method may be used only if the outcome of the contract can be reliably estimated. In the case of fixed price contracts, this degree of reliability would be provided only if all the following conditions are satisfied:**

**(a) total contract revenues to be received can be reliably estimated, and**

**(b) both the costs to complete the contract and the stage of contract performance completed at the reporting date can be reliably estimated, and**

**(c) the costs attributable to the contract can be clearly identified so that actual experience can be compared with prior estimates.**

**In the case of cost plus contracts, this degree of reliability would be provided only if both the following conditions are satisfied:**

**(a) the costs attributable to the contract can be clearly identified, and**

**(b) costs other than those that will be specifically reimbursable under the contract can be reliably estimated.**

**44. The costs included in the amount at which construction contract work is stated should comprise those costs that relate directly to a specific contract and those that are attributable to the contract activity in general and can be allocated to specific contracts.**

**45. When a contractor uses a method for a particular contract, then all other contracts that meet similar criteria should be accounted for by the same method.**

**46. A foreseeable loss on a contract should be provided for in the financial statements, both for the stage of completion reached on the contract and for future work on the contract.**

## Disclosure

**47. There should be disclosure in the financial statements of:**

**(a) the amount of construction work in progress, and**

**(b) cash received and receivable as progress payments, advances and retentions on account of contracts included in construction work in progress, and**

**(c) the amount receivable under cost plus contracts not included in construction work in progress.**

**If both the percentage of completion method and the completed contract method are simultaneously used by the contractor, the amount of contract work described in (a) above should be analysed to disclose separately the amounts attributable to contracts accounted for under each method.**

**48. Disclosure of changes in an accounting policy used for construction contracts should comply with International Accounting Standard 8, Unusual and Prior Period Items and Changes in Accounting Policies. However, if a contractor changes from the percentage of completion method to the completed contract method for contracts in progress at the beginning of the year, it may not be possible to comply with that standard and quantify the effect of the change. In such cases, disclosure should be made of the amount of attributable profits reported in prior years in respect of contracts in progress at the beginning of the accounting period.**

## Effective Date

**49. This International Accounting Standard becomes operative for financial statements covering periods beginning on or after 1 January 1980.**

# INDEX

The references are to paragraph numbers of chapters, the first number being the chapter's.